D1518186

Reading and Interpreting the Works of
TENNESSEE WILLIAMS

Enslow Publishing
101 W. 23rd Street
Suite 240
New York, NY 10011
USA
enslow.com

Lit Crit Guides

Reading and Interpreting the Works of

TENNESSEE WILLIAMS

Spring Hermann

In Memory of my mother, Margaret F. Hermann, who made me her theatre companion and devotee of the stage since childhood;
And for The Playreading Group: Betty and Herb Hoffman, Marj and Mel Johnson, Vicky and Charlie Beristain, Victor and Ruth Finizio, and my husband, Vincent, who share with me the joy of reading aloud works of great dramatic literature.

Published in 2017 by Enslow Publishing, LLC
101 W. 23rd Street, Suite 240, New York, NY 10011

Library of Congress Cataloging-in-Publication Data

Names: Hermann, Spring.
Title: Reading and interpreting the works of Tennessee Williams / Spring Hermann.
Description: New York : Enslow Publishing, 2017. | Series: Lit crit guides | Includes bibliographical references and index.
Identifiers: ISBN 9780766083462 (library bound)
Subjects: LCSH: Williams, Tennessee, 1911-1983óCriticism and interpretationóJuvenile literature.
Classification: LCC PS3545.I5365 Z677 2017 | DDC 812í.54ódc23

Printed in Malaysia

To Our Readers: We have done our best to make sure all website addresses in this book were active and appropriate when we went to press. However, the author and the publisher have no control over and assume no liability for the material available on those websites or on any websites they may link to. Any comments or suggestions can be sent by e-mail to customerservice@enslow.com.

Portions of this book originally appeared in *A Student's Guide to Tennessee Williams.*

CONTENTS

Tennessee Williams

FROM STORYTELLER TO POET TO PLAYWRIGHT: AN AUTHOR FINDS HIS CALLING

While temporarily painful, criticism . . . proves of particular benefit to a writer in the long run, especially when his aim is toward technical improvement that may eventually enable him to say things he thinks worth saying rather than toward the enjoyment of a present success. If a writer . . . has an ideal of perfection—then the ultimate outcome may be better for those initial discouragements.

—Thomas Lanier Williams, after mixed reviews of his play *Fugitive Kind*[1]

orn in 1911, Thomas Lanier Williams spent his first seven years in the Deep South. Columbia, Mississippi; Nashville, Tennessee; and Clarksdale, Mississippi were the towns where his grandfather, the Reverend Walter Dakin, served as an Episcopal priest. Tom, his older sister Rose, his mother Edwina, and his grandmother lived quietly in rectories beside Walter Dakin's churches. Tom's father, Cornelius Williams, blew in on weekends, then hit the road where he was a traveling salesman. Young Tom was sheltered in this cozy world, which was far removed from his eventual destination: the professional theater.

In 1916 Tom was stricken with diphtheria, a virulent bacterial infection that could close up the nose and throat and damage the heart, kidneys, and nervous system. There was no vaccination nor good drug treatment for diphtheria at this time, and many children died from it. Edwina and her mother struggled day and night to keep five-year-old Tom alive. Bedridden, what entertained Tom the most were the stories, poems, and songs performed for him by his mother and grandparents. The power of story to overcome pain and loneliness became embedded in Tom forever.

Cornelius moved Edwina, Rose, and Tom to St. Louis in 1918, where he became a manager at the International Shoe Company. There, a new world opened for the family. St. Louis was America's fourth largest city at the time, still robust from the World's Fair of 1903–04, and full of cultural institutions.

At best count, during the nine years that Tom spent growing up in St. Louis, the Williams family moved nine times throughout the city.[2] With Tom's baby brother Dakin in tow, Edwina dragged her children around in an obsessive quest for a roomier, more fashionable apartment. Due to a certain amount of physical weakness from diphtheria, Tom was forbidden sports or rough play. He was always the New Kid. So he found the next best thing to replace life with neighborhood pals: a life inside the world of story.

Tom eventually made a friend who felt the same way he did about living in the imagination: a sweet, red-haired girl named Hazel Kramer. From age nine through their high school years, Tom and Hazel made up games and stories, then illustrated them. In middle school, Tom had his first story published in the school paper, a piece he called "Isolated," giving him a taste of confidence and acceptance. It showed Tom's early love for melodramatic language.[3] Getting stories and poems published in school and later professional publications made Tom stand out. Always, Hazel applauded his efforts. Tom thought of Hazel as his first real love.

Physically, Tom was slender and short in stature like his mother. His father never understood him and sometimes called him "Miss Nancy." Edwina referred to Tom as her writer son and supported his efforts with a new typewriter. This further angered Tom's father, who believed writers were an odd bunch that never made any money. The wedge between Cornelius and Tom grew, as did the constant quarreling between Cornelius and Edwina.

One thing that Cornelius did provide were summer visits with his sisters, Tom's two affectionate aunts. Isabel "Belle" Brownlow and Ella Williams of Knoxville, Tennessee, adored Tom. Aunt Belle taught him to swim, his favorite exercise for life. Tom and Rose gained a sense of freedom with their Tennessee friends. Rose, then a rebellious teen, often got her younger brother Tom involved in schemes with her pals. Later, the aunts would introduce Rose socially in their city, hoping to settle her down with a suitable boy.

College Student

In 1929, at age eighteen, Tom headed off to the University of Missouri in Columbia. Tom wrote to his grandparents: "Mother is going up with me to spend one day to see that I am properly settled. She acts as though I were leaving for war instead of college."[4] The School of Journalism was what mainly attracted Tom, as well as the distance between the true war zone of his life: the one that existed in his own home.

Tom pledged Alpha Tau Omega fraternity, went out for wrestling at which he had some skill, and quickly found his way into writing and literature courses. The one requirement—Reserved Officers Training Course—was the sticking point for Tom. He hated its weaponry and regulations. Tom's ATO brothers knew he was different in many ways—some called him untidy, absent-minded, and oddball. Yet they admitted he was a good dancer, a hit at mixers with sororities, and nicknamed him Tiger.

In 1930, Tom bumped into an endeavor that attracted him: playwriting. The university's "Missouri Workshop one-act play contest" enticed Tom to try his first dramatic work. The result, *Beauty Is the Word*, was Tom's first play—and although it only won sixth place, it was the first freshman entry ever to medal. Only the first place winner got money and a production. From that moment on, Tom was hooked on playwriting—and determined to be the one who got the money!

During his three years at the University of Missouri, Tom enjoyed reading a wide variety of literature, learning to write poetry and short plays, and drinking with his frat brothers. His ATO roommate for a term was Harold Mitchell. Tom developed a deep fondness for Mitch, how deep he could not understand at that time. Mitch recalled many years later: "I liked Tom—he was a very nice guy—but there was never anything between us but good friendship. I didn't know he was gay, and I don't really believe he knew he was either."[5] Being openly homosexual at that time would have meant expulsion from ATO and probably from the university. Mitch admitted Tom was "a hell of a lot better writer than I was. He had worlds of talent but I would have never predicted his success."[6]

When the great economic depression of the 1930s hit the nation, Tom's family survived but money was extremely tight in their household. With Tom's grades falling below his potential, and his failure to pass ROTC three times, Cornelius forced Tom to quit school after his junior year and go to work.

In a time of huge unemployment, Tom was hired as a clerk at International Shoe for sixty-five dollars a month, only because his father made it happen. His years at menial labor, while miserable and boring, taught him a great deal about the lives of others. He recalled later "I learned about the comradeship between co-workers at minimum salary, and I made some very good friends."[7] One was a Polish fellow named Stanley Kowalski.

At night, with his remaining energy, Tom worked on short stories and plays, then entered them in contests. He had received letters from the university faculty, expressing regret he had to drop out, encouraging him to keep trying to publish his writing. Lonely, with most of his contemporaries working or at university, Tom became a model of perseverance. Tirelessly he submitted his work, often winning, sometimes even earning prize money. One special event happened in 1934 that impacted on his future life. He saw a performance at a St. Louis theater of *Ghosts* by Henrik Ibsen. The powerful acting amazed him. The forbidden subject matter of inherited venereal disease astounded him. He stated that it was "one of the things that made me want to write for the theatre."[8]

Tom Williams was a poor worker for International Shoe. His lack of focus caused him to lose orders. He stayed up nights drinking coffee, reading, and writing. Stress over his writing career, poor nutrition, and hidden anxiety about his uncertain sexual orientation, took its toll. In early 1935, he had something he called a "cardiac seizure." He said that a doctor told him that "I did indeed have a defective heart."[9] Tom's father became so concerned, that, Tom said, "For my twenty-fourth birthday I received a permanent release from the wholesale shoe business." [10]

Tom stands with his grandmother, Rose, and grandfather, the Reverend Walter Dakin, with whom he lived for much of his childhood and had a close relationship.

Tom spent the following summer resting with his grand-parents. During that time he befriended a neighbor, Dorothy Shapiro, who belonged to a community theater group. Together they assembled *Cairo! Shanghai! Bombay!*, a comedy in four scenes. To Tom's delight, Dorothy's group, the Garden Players, put on their play. To hear laughter and applause for his work, to see actors glowing and accepting him as their playwright—was amazing. Tom wrote in his *Memoirs*: "Then and there the theatre and I found each other for better and for worse."[11]

The Williams family resided on Pershing Avenue in University City, very near the campus of Washington University. Edwina and her parents scraped up the money to pay tuition for extension classes at this famous school, which allowed Tom to return to the study of writing. It was here that Tom began writing long plays. However, after finishing his extension courses, he was advised to return to a university with a good theater department that would accept all his previous credits. The State University of Iowa in Iowa City fit the bill. They actually offered a degree in Experimental Dramatic Production. Tom knew there would be stiff competition from ambitious young writers—but he was ready to excel.

LOCAL BOY MAKES GOOD!

Not long after arriving in Iowa, Williams rushed back to St. Louis during the fall of 1937 for an important reason. His new play was "going up," to the delight of his family, friends, and community. The Mummers of St. Louis, a community theater, would present the premiere of *Fugitive Kind* by Thomas Lanier Williams. The play would have two performances, Tuesday, November 30, and Saturday, December 4, 1937, in the Wednesday Club Auditorium.

The Mummers had also done Williams's first play, *Candles to the Sun*, in January 1937. This production about downtrodden coal miners used the sun to symbolize group consciousness and labor-union power. It was not a play that remained popular but was considered "a local success."[12] It encouraged the Mummers to believe Williams was a fine writer of realistic social drama.

Men stand in a soup line during the depression in the 1930s. Like so many Americans, Tom's family struggled financially during this time, an experience he used in his early writing.

Williams had finished the draft of *Fugitive Kind*, his second full-length play, in September, just before he started his theater studies in Iowa City. When he left, he wrote in his journal about *Fugitive Kind*: "My play is all but finished and I feel pretty well satisfied with it. Now I yearn for work on a new one. . . . The next play is always the important play. . . . I want to go on creating. I will!"[13]

Tom wanted to bring common troubled people to life in his work. Most of the characters in *Fugitive Kind* were homeless, holed up in a cheap transient hotel called a flophouse. Williams actually explored some of these flophouses to gain a true perspective. The Depression of the 1930s and the unsympathetic large corporations had forced millions of Americans into marginal lives. The characters in *Fugitive Kind* exemplified these people, who also lived with the threat of crime and the presence of robbers on the run. Williams knew that his audiences would relate to desperate people, even law breakers. Criminals were almost folk heroes during the Depression.

In his play, Williams introduced a large cast of twenty-five diverse individuals. Many of these characters were briefly seen and provided background material. Others were deeply portrayed. All of his characters had a style of speaking that perfectly suited their role in life. He even spelled out the European Jewish accent one character needed when writing his speeches. These characters spoke using internal

monologue (internal or interior)

A long speech by an individual character in which he lets the audience alone know his inner thoughts and feelings.

monologue (external or exterior)

A long speech by an individual character, sometimes in the presence of other characters, that reveals his past or planned actions and intentions.

and external monologues. Some of these monologues were more poetic than realistic.

Metaphor and Symbol Are Interwoven in Realistic Drama

Williams began to transfer his poetic impulses to his dramas. For him, a metaphor meant that locales and events stood for something else. In *Fugitive Kind*, his homeless characters move in and out of Gwendlebaum's flophouse for fifteen cents a night. He located the flophouse near the banks of the Mississippi by the Eads Bridge. This famous suspension bridge symbolizes St. Louis as a gateway to the Golden West. It also acts as a fast way out of town, the way to get from a bad place to a better one. Williams himself was trying to use his playwriting as a bridge to get out of a dreary life with his oppressive parents into a world where he could achieve. However, he also used the Eads Bridge as a site for an attempted suicide for Leo, a good but confused character in his play.

Williams used the metaphor of snow, which looks white and pure and beautiful, covering up the mud of the world. His homeless characters also realize this same snow can freeze you to death. The regular ringing of a nearby cathedral's bells marks the passage of time. The tolling of bells also symbolizes a march toward a dark, inevitable fate. The use of metaphoric locales and events with double interpretations would continue through Williams's works.

Relationships Seen in a New Light

Another subject that Williams explored in *Fugitive Kind* was sexual attraction between characters. In the 1930s, frank portrayal of people's sexual lives was not often seen on stage. Glory, the heroine of the play, is torn between two men.

One is her safe, undemanding boyfriend, Herman. The other is Terry, a man on the run from a bank robbery. Terry is powerful, lonely, and appealing, so Glory is hopelessly drawn to him. When the desire between them become overwhelming, Glory succumbs to Terry sexually. She then plans their escape before the law catches him.

Williams continued to develop fascinating female characters. His radical "modern" women with their own needs, mindsets, and sexual desires would stand up to their male counterparts. As seen in the character of Glory, passion may cause women to make self-destructive mistakes. Yet Williams's female characters would follow their own impulsive drives.

metaphor
An implied comparison achieved by using a word or phrase not in its literal sense, but as an analogy. Example (from Shakespeare): "Life's but a walking shadow, a poor player that struts and frets his hour upon the stage."

symbol
Something that stands for, represents, or suggests another thing.

symbolism
The representation of things by use of symbols.

Nature vs Nurture: Becoming Who We Are

In *Fugitive Kind*, Terry the criminal talks about the way childhood traumas and genetics influence the way we turn out as adults. In scene 5, Terry tells Glory that his mother became a prostitute and got tuberculosis. As for his father, Terry tells Glory: "Maybe if my old man hadn't caught a steel rivet between the eyes when I was ten months old, I'd have turned out to be Herman."[14] In *Fugitive Kind*, Williams indicates that early nurturing seems a stronger way to determine behavior than genetics.

WILLIAMS AND POETRY

Williams stated that he admired the poetry of D. H. Lawrence, Walt Whitman, Emily Dickinson, and especially Hart Crane. These poets were all considered passionate, lyrical writers. The term *lyrical poet* means that the writer's stanzas are flowing and musical, like a song. Lyrical poetry expresses the writer's deep, personal feelings and emotions. Williams transferred his poetic impulses to his works for the stage, where his characters sang, as did the lyrical poet, the dilemmas of the human heart.

Favorite Poetic Writers in Williams's Life

D. H. Lawrence (1885–1930)—British novelist and poet known for frankly exploring human need and sexual relationships.

Emily Dickinson (1830–1886)—Massachusetts author of 1,800 poems, famed for her innovative use of meter, metaphors, and subjects.

Hart Crane (1899–1932)—Ohio-born poet and modernist who struggled with his homosexuality within his role as a writer. Williams's favorite.

Walt Whitman (1819–1892)—New York poet-journalist known for his experimental free verse.

Tom was drawn to the poetry of Hart Crane at an early age. Crane, pictured here, was a tragic literary figure who ended his own life at thirty-two, but whose works expressed beauty and optimism in the modern world.

Alternative Dramatic Speaking Styles

Terry delivers his feelings in an interior monologue. This device of a character revealing his inner thoughts allowed Williams to infuse poetry and emotion into ordinary speech. Terry also delivers exterior monologues to explain his situation. The other characters on stage, as well as the audience, could decide how they felt about the speaker. These techniques, often used in poetry and stories, would be effective in Williams's future plays.

In one of the stage directions in *Fugitive Kind*, Williams tells the director: "Chuck's speeches will remain upon the realistic plane, but Leo's will really be passages of poetry and will have to be delivered as such."[15] The use of poetic dialogue would become a Williams trademark.

The Artist Against the Industrial World

The theme of what poets, artists, and performers, even dreamers, had to do to survive in America's business-oriented society was one close to Williams's heart. Glory's brother, Leo, does not fit into routine corporate work. He says: "Why don't I belong out there with the rest of those people? . . . The only thing I'm good for, Chuck, is putting words down on paper. And what's the use of that?"[16]

Tom Williams examined the idea of dual realities. One reality would be a situation as seen by the average working person. The second reality would be the same situation as perceived by the artistic dreamer. Which view of the situation is more "real"?

Questioning the Power of Faith

Williams explores the relationship between God and mankind in *Fugitive Kind*. His grandfather Reverend Dakin, and his mother, Edwina, taught a firm Christianity to him and his siblings. Yet Williams often wondered aloud in his writing whether God really cared. So many people seemed to suffer needlessly. A character in *Fugitive Kind* describes a world going to war while "God's asleep." A search for spiritual meaning would be made by many of Williams's characters. Later, guilt and the quest for salvation would become a recurring theme in his plays.

realism

A style of writing in which the subject is represented as it would be in real life.

theme

A distinctive quality or concern in one or more works of fiction.

Another theme of his was only touched upon in *Fugitive Kind*: the effect of depression and mental illness. Abel White, a transient, is a dangerous psychopath who starts fires. Glory's brother, Leo, an intense college student, becomes obsessed with Socialist politics. When the state of the world overwhelms him, Leo almost commits suicide. This theme of depression reoccurs in several major plays.

While waiting for the Mummers's opening performance of *Fugitive Kind*, Williams himself became depressed. He had been promised a set that would show the oppressive city skyline and the falling snow through a huge window. This set did not materialize. His characters did not look like fugitives crowded together in their last refuge. He had been in Iowa City during most of the rehearsals, when the playwright should have been present for revisions. Williams feared that no one would understand the play's meaning. Nerves, fright, and loneliness devastated him on opening night.

A cast member of *Fugitive Kind*, Jane Garret Carter, recalled a darkly comic moment before the show opened.

Carter said, "We were in the dressing room, and suddenly Tom ran to the window and said, 'Jane, I'm going to jump.' I grabbed him and said, 'Listen to me, Tom Williams, you'd have to go head first, because it's only one story down and you'll just break your leg.'"[17]

Response to Criticism Makes the Writer

Williams endured his opening night. The St. Louis critics were mixed, but all said that *Fugitive Kind* needed revision. They called Williams's work exciting, new, vital, and colorful. Yet Williams was groping for his personal style of expression. If he was going to become a successful and innovative playwright, he would have to find this style and stay true to it.

Williams knew he had to work harder, revise more, and master his structural problems. It did not matter what was inside his head—only what he conveyed to his audience members. His characters had to express the author's story. It was their speeches, actions, tears, and dreams that counted. Williams would always be stung by criticism. Then he would turn around and use it toward revision and strengthening of his work. His greatest plays would be revised many times. This ideal of perfection became so high that he continued revising some of his works until he died.

From Tom to Tennessee

Thomas Lanier Williams did not become Tennessee Williams until after he graduated from the University of Iowa. He claimed that when he lived in the Alpha Tau Omega fraternity house during his senior year in Iowa City, the fellows decided he had a Southern accent. His speech sounded funny to their Midwestern ears. He recalled that his frat brothers settled on Tennessee for his nickname, although he had only spent one year (plus summers) in that state. Williams had been looking for a way to stand out and be memorable. When he started to send plays to contests and agents in New York, he began to use the name Tennessee Williams. It was a name that people definitely remembered.

Maxwell Anderson, Lillian Hellman, Sidney Howard, Clifford Odets, William Saroyan, and Eugene O'Neill were the big Broadway playwrights of the 1930s. Tennessee Williams's dramas were different from any of their plays, unique in style and context. He would have to find his own path as a playwright and the courage to stick to it.

Williams's Amazing Body of Work

According to most chronologies, Williams had twenty-four full-length plays produced in his lifetime. Some were not successful or enduring. Others, such as *The Glass Menagerie, A Streetcar Named Desire, The Rose Tattoo, Camino Real, Cat on a Hot Tin Roof, Garden District* [*Something Unspoken* and *Suddenly Last Summer*], *Sweet Bird of Youth, The Night of the Iguana, Period of Adjustment, The Milk Train Doesn't Stop Here Anymore, Summer and Smoke,* and *Small Craft Warnings,* were widely produced, and are regularly revived today. Williams won the New York Drama Critics' Circle award four times, the Pulitzer Prize twice, the Donaldson Award, the Sidney Howard Memorial Award, and the Tony Award for Best Play during his life as a playwright.

Williams wrote many one-act plays, which are usually produced in groupings. He also penned six short-story collections, two volumes of poetry, and two novels. Top screenwriters turned Williams's plays into fifteen films. Williams acted as screenwriter on seven of them. All were considered successful, and some received Academy Awards. Some of

Williams's dramas returned as original film productions on television. Many talented actors played the leads in Tennessee Williams's plays on both the stage and the screen. Williams's work boosted the careers of stage and film directors, actors, and designers. The number and importance of Williams's plays rival that of any other American dramatist.

Building a Playwright's Résumé: Tom's Search for Work and a Home

As Williams worked to find his identity as a writer, his sister, Rose, was descending into mental illness. Not only was Rose obsessed with attracting men and defying her mother, her behavior sometimes turned destructive, requiring hospitalization. Williams wrote that "Love's explosion" in his schizophrenic sister "consumingly shone in her transparent heart for a season / And burned it out, a tissue-paper lantern."[1] This image may remind readers of Blanche Dubois in *A Streetcar Named Desire* and that character's similarly fragile state. Tom always loved Rose—but could not save her. He spent most of 1939 on the West Coast, working, writing, and thinking about his sister whom he could not help.

Although Williams finished his college degree in August 1938 at age twenty-seven, he was not equipped to earn a living at anything but writing. He tried to get a job on a Works Progress Administration (WPA) project. The WPA was the name of a group of government agencies set up to give jobs to the nation's 10 million unemployed, beginning in 1935. One of the WPA's agencies was called the Federal Writers' Project and another one was the Federal Theatre Project. The WPA had an office located in New Orleans, where Williams traveled to get work. In 1938, he found the city's French Quarter was filled with bars, brothels, artists, and musicians. "I've never known anybody who lived in . . . the Quarter who wasn't slightly intoxicated—without booze," Williams observed.[2] New Orleans was his kind of town.

An Itinerant Lifestyle

Williams's practice of observing and absorbing peoples' lives and conversations had begun in his youth. In New Orleans, he

The French Quarter of New Orleans is every bit as vibrant today as it was in Williams's time. He referred to the city as his "spiritual home" and set several of his novels there.

inhaled the culture eagerly. The sexual freedom of the French Quarter allowed him to face his growing feelings of homosexuality. Here he would send out plays using the Tennessee Williams pen name. Since the WPA job never came through, he lived on scraps, part-time jobs with restaurants, and handouts from his family. He set up his lifelong plan of rising early, writing steadily through most of the day, and, after a swim (if possible), cruising and partying through the evening.

During the next few nomadic years, Williams lived in California, St. Louis, New York, Provincetown on Cape Cod, and Key West, Florida. As he drifted, he hung onto his typewriter and a trunk of drafts, exploring his themes and characters. When he wrote short stories or one-act plays, he did not necessarily intend them to be sketches or short parts of a major play. Yet he seemed to take characters, themes, actions, and motifs from his short works and use them as inspiration for his long ones.

The Short Works

The Trinity Repertory Company, a professional theater in Providence, Rhode Island, produced a performance of readings of Williams's one-act plays on October 29, 2005. Director Laura Kepley spoke at this performance about why Williams's short works are important. "In these short plays, you see prototypes of great characters he created," she said. They also provide a window into "the world of imagination he constructs."[3]

The following plays were chosen by Kepley and the Trinity Rep cast. Published before 1945, the year Williams had his first hit with *The Glass Menagerie*, they predate this great play plus his *Battle of Angels*. Williams's genius shines in bright short flashes, helping us to follow his growth as a writer.

The Lady of Larkspur Lotion

In this darkly comic work, Williams writes about his poor days in New Orleans's French Quarter. He introduces two renters of small ugly rooms on the edge of society. The Landlady (Mrs. Wire) is hard on both the Lady (Mrs. Hardwicke-Moore) and her neighbor the Writer, who owe her rent. The Lady maintains high-tone airs, dreams, and fantasies about support coming in from a Brazilian admirer. The Landlady knows that the little money the Lady gets is from men she entertains in her room. The Larkspur Lotion that the lady clings to is really cheap alcohol. Mrs. Wire calls both of them "Quarter rats, half-breeds, drunks, degenerates, who try to get by on promises, lies, delusions!"[4]

The Writer defends the Lady, and shouts at the landlady: "Suppose I wanted to be a great artist but lacked the force and the power? Suppose the curtains of my exalted fancy rose on magnificent dramas—but the house-lights darkened before the curtain fell!"[5] After ejecting the Landlady, the Writer confesses he likes to be called Mr. Chekhov. His compassion allows the Lady to dream on for another day.

The Lady is a precursor of Blanche DuBois of *A Streetcar Named Desire* in her attitudes, faded Southern gentility, and hidden sexuality. The Writer expresses Williams's own belief that artists need their dreams to escape from the hard cold lies of the real world.

Hello from Bertha

This play offers an outstanding yet demanding role for a middle-aged actress. Bertha, an aging prostitute from the river flats of East St. Louis, is too exhausted mentally and emotionally to decide what to do with herself. The brothel's madam, called Goldie, wants Bertha to work or get out of the room. She needs it for other business. The tension that grows between Goldie and Bertha is gripping, yet darkly amusing. Soon Bertha's fantasies are more real to her than her sordid life. She suffers from severe alcoholism and paranoia. Goldie knows Bertha needs hospitalization. Claiming Goldie will lock her up in "the city bug house," Bertha's moods flash from sentimental love for Charlie, the man she once worked for as a girl, to fury over a supposed robbery. Williams in his stage direction describes Bertha's condition as "schizophrenic suspicion."[6]

Another prostitute, Lena, comes in to check on Bertha, as she moves in and out of lucidity. Bertha dictates to Lena a letter, which simply says: "Hello from Bertha to Charlie—with all her love."[7]

Williams, when a college student, went with some pals to the East St. Louis brothels. The stark realism of Bertha's situation is drawn from his own observations. Williams's sister, Rose, was already mentally ill around the time this piece was written. Several of Williams's major characters echo Bertha in their delusions and desperation, in plays that became classics.

This Property Is Condemned

Williams depicts a thirteen-year-old scarecrow of a girl named Willie who is found wandering the railroad tracks. A fourteen-year-old boy called Tom, who has cut school to fly his kite, encounters the girl and listens as she relates her bizarre tale. She longs for her dead older sister, Alva, whom she adored. Wearing her sister's old velvet dress, Willie claims she will take over Alva's male admirers, the railroad men who slept with her. The child's odd perceptions, lack of values, and abandonment by her family become frightening. Yet Willie's perky personality gives us hope for her.

Like *The Lady of Larkspur Lotion*, *This Property* has offbeat humor. Willie is barely surviving on handouts and garbage, living in a condemned house. Yet her spirit and spunk never fail her. Williams captures the voice of an adolescent Delta country girl, a voice he never used again. The sense of abandonment, however, is explored by characters in later plays. The screenplay of this piece was produced in 1966, when young Francis Ford Coppola wrote the expanded script.

Williams uses repeated poetic images in *This Property Is Condemned*, which he will do again in larger works. Willie and Tom repeat the image of the sky as being "perfectly white. It's white as a clean piece of paper."[8] Willie also recalls her fifth-grade teacher giving her a "white piece of paper," to make a drawing. But Willie draws her own dark reality, her father being hit with a whiskey bottle. Willie recalls the image of white when she tells Tom her dying sister dreamed of getting "loads and loads of white flowers," like Greta Garbo got as Camille. Now Alva is in "the bone-orchard." The whiteness of bones completes the imagery, for whiteness is the symbol of hope, purity, and death.

The Unsatisfactory Supper

Also titled *The Long Stay Cut Short*, this brief piece tells the tale of Aunt Rose, the aged servant, and her employers. Sharp jabs between the married couple Baby Doll and Archie Lee, with sly additions by Rose, create stress in this Delta drama. Aunt Rose has been passed around the family like a piece of property. Now no one wants her because she cannot even boil greens properly.

Aunt Rose can be arch, dry, and humorous and holds her own with Baby and Archie Lee. At the end, Aunt Rose moves into senility, panic, and symbolically dies, blowing away in

Natalie Wood and Robert Redford play the roles of Alva and Owen in the 1966 film *This Property Is Condemned*.

the wind. She echoes some of Williams's family members, including Ozzie, Tom's story-telling nanny; his elderly grandmother; and his sister, Rose, the most beloved people in Tom's world, who became unwelcome annoyances in Cornelius Williams's home.

Sometimes Williams took a character and an incident in a short play, and incorporated them into a larger work. For instance, his play *27 Wagons Full of Cotton* features Silva Vicarro, the superintendent of the Syndicate Plantation in Blue Mountain, Mississippi. Vicarro has a large load of cotton to process. His cotton gin was mysteriously burned. So he must pay to use the one owned by Jake, the man we know was responsible for the arson. Jake's wife, Flora, keeps Vicarro "entertained" all day while Jake does the job. In his full-length screenplay, *Baby Doll* (1956), Williams used the Silva Vicarro character and the burning of the gin, but created a different direction to the story. He also radically changed Flora and created a servant similar to Aunt Rose.

A production of Williams's short plays called *8 by Tenn* was done in 2003 by the Hartford Stage, Hartford, Connecticut. The program covered two evenings. Critic Karen Bovard wrote of these short works: "While many of them would be unsatisfying in isolation, together they offer a rare glimpse into the experimental variety Williams favored and for which he rarely receives credit."[9]

Surviving the Hungry, Lonely Years

The road Tennessee Williams traveled from starving writer in New Orleans in 1939 to nationally recognized playwright in 1945 was an uphill climb. In 1939, Williams won a prize from the Group Theatre in New York—one hundred dollars for three one-act plays. In order to enter this competition for relative beginners, Tennessee decided to become three years younger than Tom Williams. The judges of this contest sent his one-acts to a fine theatrical agent, Audrey Wood, who reviewed Williams's work and saw a special talent. Wood helped him apply for a further grant. The Dramatist Guild, through a grant from the Rockefeller Foundation, awarded him a writing fellowship of one thousand dollars by the end of 1939.[10]

Although the funds kept him going as he moved from town to town, Williams was still sad. After visiting his sister during a stay at a Missouri mental hospital, he confessed in his journal that he felt guilty he could not share even a bit of his success with her. He called her beyond the reach of joy.

The "Big Break" in Boston

Battle of Angels, Williams's first full professional production, was put on by the Theatre Guild in Boston from December 20, 1940, to January 11, 1941. The story of the handsome drifter Val and his potent, erotic effect on the married storekeeper Myra, the wealthy, alcoholic Sandra, the artistic Vee, and other women of a small Southern town, was boldly, poetically told. The characters and plot contained many underlying references to both the New Testament story of Christ and the Greek myth of Odysseus. The Boston critics were confused, unimpressed, and

Group Theatre

Formed in 1931 in New York, this company held left-wing political views and produced plays that explored social issues.

Dramatist Guild of America

Organization that promotes and protects the professional interests of playwrights, composers, lyricists, and librettists.

put off by its frank sexuality. To Williams's dismay, the play closed.

During the period of 1942 to 1943, Tennessee Williams was broke again. He begged for rooms and meals from friends, moving from city to city, beach to beach. He was forced to return to his parents at times if only to take a bath and sleep in a bed. In 1943, Williams was on the road again, heading for a Hollywood studio that hired him to do screen writing. In January, his mother had written him that his sister, Rose, who had been a patient at a state mental hospital for six years, had been given a prefrontal lobotomy. This radical brain surgery frightened Williams, but he could do nothing about Rose at that time. He needed the Hollywood job, mainly for the money. But no matter how much the studio paid, Williams found he could not write much except what came from his heart.

Williams's agent, Audrey Wood, understood the playwright well. Without Wood, Williams might never have had

A CONTROVERSIAL TREATMENT

The frontal lobotomy, or leucotomy, is a neurosurgical operation that involves severing connections in the brain's prefrontal lobe. Widely performed to treat schizophrenia, manic depression/bipolar disorder, and other mental illnesses, it is estimated that fifty thousand of these procedures were done in the 1930s to the 1980s. Most patients were not "cured" and lost their personality. Rose Williams would need residential care for the rest of her life (much like another famous patient, Rosemary Kennedy, the US president's sister). Although electroconvulsive therapy is still used, most of today's psychiatric patients are treated with more effective pharmaceuticals.

Williams's long-time agent, Audrey Wood, ran an agency in partnership with her husband, William Liebling (in frame above Wood). She was often one of the first to read Wiliams's completed drafts and offered the playwright valuable feedback and advice.

the career he did. She represented him as an author and also took care of such personal matters as his draft classification card. She wrote to him in 1942: "I'm keeping the original because if I sent it to you, you might lose it."[11] Williams was classified 4F. This meant his physical problems—his bad eyesight and heart—kept him from being drafted for combat in World War II.

A long-awaited miracle arrived for Williams late in 1944. During 1940, he had begun a draft of a play called *Stairs to the Roof*. It partly concerned a young aspiring poet stuck working in a shoe factory. Williams took elements of this play, then added the writer's mother and sister to the plot. Incorporating additional material from some of his short stories, as well as his personal life, Williams named this new play *The Gentleman Caller*. He tried to sell it to the Hollywood studio as a screenplay, but failed. Again he reworked it as a stage play, now calling it *The Glass Menagerie*. This version struck gold with a New York producer. Revolutionary in style, concept, and structure, this play would make Tennessee Williams famous.

The Glass Menagerie: A Family Crystalized

The first production of *The Glass Menagerie* opened in Chicago on December 26, 1944, starring Laurette Taylor as Amanda Wingfield and Eddie Dowling as Tom. Williams said, "No one knew how to take *Menagerie*, it was something of an innovation in the theatre."[12] In fact, it was different from Williams's first major plays, *Fugitive Kind* and *Battle of Angels*, lacking their sharpness and social commentary. It had little sexual interchange and no violence. In 1965, the author told the *New York Times* that on his last typed version of this play, he wrote: "*The Glass Menagerie*, a rather dull little play by

Tennessee Williams."[13] As the play was closing its first run in Chicago and moving to New York, its star Laurette Taylor said to Williams: "Do you think Broadway, this bastardly place, will buy this lovely delicate fragile little thing?"[14]

The play's action was simple. A middle-aged mother, deserted by her husband, depends on her restless adult son and is devoted to her reclusive adult daughter. Her goal is to keep the family together financially and emotionally during hard times. The son's goal is to break his ties to his mother and sister and seek adventure in the world. The action takes place in the Wingfields' cramped St. Louis apartment and on its fire escape. This story, partly drawn from Williams's short story called "Portrait of a Girl in Glass," is a nostalgic, painful series of memories in which the narrator recreates his family. These characters' moods and feelings are more important than an active plot line. Emotional journeys take precedence over physical action. *The Glass Menagerie* captures the love, frustration, compassion, and human weakness that all families experience.

> **Theatre Guild**
>
> Founded in 1919 in New York, this producing group was owned by its board of directors, which included playwrights, actors, and designers. It was noted for giving new authors a chance to develop. Some younger radical members broke away and formed the Group Theatre.

To give the sense of movement back through time into memory, Williams wanted to use unusual scenic effects, projected slides, mysterious lighting [in one scene the audience joined Laura and Jim lit only by candlelight], and an emotional musical score. Composer Paul Bowles was surprised when approached, since non-musical productions seldom had scores. He said about the new script: "I read it and liked it," although he admitted it was "somewhat experimental" for

Broadway. The producers apparently allowed the music at the last minute, because Bowles said "I found myself with three days in which to compose and orchestrate the score."[15]

Time and Reality Take On New Dimensions

In *Glass Menagerie*, Tom Wingfield, the adult son, is also the narrator of the play. He says he is giving us "truth in the pleasant disguise of illusion." This lets us know that the truth may be painful. Tom explains that the play is taking place in his memory. Happenings may not be presented realistically because memory is seated in the heart.

We do not learn how many actual years have passed between the "present" of Tom the narrator and the "past" of the family's life together. The characters and incidents are crystallized, captured in the moments they shared. For each character, time has a different meaning. For the Son, time has been stalled. All he wants is to break free and get into forward motion. For the Daughter, time is slowly creeping. She would like to stop time altogether and live in the protected frozen world of her glass collection. For the Mother, time has already passed. All she can do is cling to her control of the family and remember. Her chance to have a comfortable, loving relation-ship with a man seems over. For the Gentleman Caller, time is roaring ahead. He grabs on to its tail and rushes into the world of the future.

Williams blends all four characters and their different perceptions into a single frame. He wrote his ideas about the nature of time and reality while working on this play. "The only reality . . . that has form and dimension is the one that exists in recollection. Now is formless, now is almost breathless, now is something too little even to measure."[16] Williams means that we can only really know something that has already passed.

The present is too fast to capture or reflect upon. However, he does allow his characters to have their own reality.

Characters Imbued with Williams's Family Memories

By the time *The Glass Menagerie* opened, Williams was thirty-three years old. He had been writing steadily since he was an adolescent. Sometimes he preferred to go hungry and homeless rather than take a meaningless day job. He said he was "a compulsive typist and a compulsive writer . . . that's my life . . . my intense life is my work."[17] One of the few jobs he was forced to take was in the offices and warehouse of the International Shoe Company.

Tom Wingfield, the Son in *Menagerie*, is also forced to work at the local shoe company. He escapes by writing poetry on shoe boxes and going to the movies. Tom loves his sister but cannot really help her. He respects his mother but cannot stand daily life with her. Desperate for travel and adventure to feed his creativity, he is much like the young Tom Williams. However, there was an important difference in Williams's life. In the play, the Father has taken off years before, giving the Son a model of escape. Williams had to contend with his real father. Cornelius Williams did live at home and supported the family. He fought often with his wife, openly disliked his older son, Tom, and disapproved of his daughter.

Laura Wingfield suffers from a slight physical disability that causes her to limp. Her nervous, shy, introverted personality makes her a failure socially. Laura's ability to hold a business position or attract a husband fades as she moves into a private world. Tom Williams, during the years he lived at home after college, recalled his sister's white room with its shelves of miniature glass animals as a refuge. Williams said in

The original Broadway production of *The Glass Menagerie* opened in 1945. It starred (left to right) Anthony Ross as Jim O'Connor, Laurette Taylor as Amanda Wingfield, Eddie Dowling as Tom, and Julie Haydon as Laura.

an interview: "[H]er glass menagerie had a meaning for me. The glass animals came to represent the fragile, delicate ties that must be broken . . . when you try to fulfill yourself."[18]

Rose Williams had a different set of problems than Laura Wingfield presents. Rose's lively charm and good looks had attracted men. However, her overwrought personality and emotional imbalance kept suitors from proposing marriage. Rose was also too nervous to work in business. Unlike Laura Wingfield, Rose Williams was sexually discontent and became increasingly violent.

Amanda Wingfield, the Mother, may be the character closest to her Williams family counterpart. Amanda's life centers on running her home and her children's lives. She can be demanding and dramatic and a frantically lively talker. She is proud to be an officer in the St. Louis Daughters of the American Revolution. She is clever at economizing. Memories of her youth filled with parties and suitors in her Mississippi community are recounted to her children. When we meet her in her late forties, Amanda is clinging to a charm that is fading like the Old South. In these ways, she is a reflection of Edwina Dakin Williams.

A major break in reality between Amanda Wingfield and Edwina Williams occurs when Williams removes the husband/ father figure from the home. Mr. Wingfield's desertion deeply affects Amanda, Laura, and Tom. All Father leaves behind is a large smiling portrait. When Tom explodes at Amanda for taking away his books by D. H. Lawrence (the British novelist and poet whom Williams said he idolized), he tells her: "If self is what I thought of, Mother, I'd be where he is—GONE! [He points to his father's picture.] As far as the system of transportation reaches!"[19] Williams believed that in one way his own father was "absent" and that was emotionally. Cornelius never

41

made him feel that he loved his children, except his youngest, Dakin. In his twenties, Williams said that he thought he was important only to his father "because I was the namesake of his own father, Thomas Lanier Williams II."[20]

In its earlier versions, *The Glass Menagerie* was called *The Caller* or *The Gentleman Caller*. This may seem strange, since the character of the Gentleman Caller, named Jim O'Connor, is an outsider. The Gentleman Caller was very important to the author, however. He portrayed the average ambitious workingman. Tom says of Jim that he is the emissary from the world of reality, a place from which the Wingfield family is set apart. Jim has never been the poet or the dreamer. He is the popular fellow Laura adored from afar in high school. Amanda sees him as representing the future American. She hopes he is a link to a prosperous life for Laura. Tom Wingfield says that "like some archetype of the universal unconscious, the image of the gentleman caller haunted our small apartment . . ."[21]

As the play ends, the only character with a defined, achievable goal outside his present situation is Jim O'Connor. He has already found a girl to marry, a fact that Tom never realized when he brought him to dinner. Amanda and Laura are totally unprepared to succeed in the postwar half of the twentieth century. Tom's goal is to escape the corporate grind. He takes the money needed to pay the electric bill and uses it to join the Merchant Marine. Trying to break his attachment to his sister, Tom says he "followed, from then on, in my father's footsteps, attempting to find in motion what was lost in space."[22]

Family Pressures Propel the Play

Williams continued to study the effect of childhood trauma on his adult characters. In the Wingfield family, each character is shaped by loss. Amanda has lost the romantic possibilities of marrying well and living the pampered life she was raised to expect. Amanda's family gave her no realistic way to support herself.

Laura tries to be the girl her mother needs at home, but out in the world, she is a solitary loner. Laura deeply loves her brother and mother, and tries to keep the peace between them, yet cannot meet their needs and expectations. Jim the Gentleman Caller says to her regarding their high school days: "[Y]ou had this inferiority complex that keeps you from feeling comfortable with people. Somebody needs to build your confidence up and make you proud instead of shy and turning away . . .".[23]

Tom is the most obviously affected by family stress. He cannot replace his runaway father, nor can he stand his mother's nagging and suspicions. Claiming his enemies plan to dynamite their apartment, Tom shouts: "You'll go up, up on a broomstick, over Blue Mountain with seventeen gentlemen callers! You ugly—babbling old—witch!"[24] Later as he apologizes, Tom tells Amanda she cannot know what is inside his heart.

Themes of Loss, Loneliness, and the Limitations of Reality

In a 1948 interview, Tennessee Williams said: "For me the dominating premise has been the need for understanding and tenderness and fortitude among individuals trapped by circumstances."[25] In other interviews, Williams discussed human loneliness as being a major theme in his writing.

All of the Wingfields are trapped by circumstance and unfulfilled need. The emotional climax of the play, states Professor Roger Boxill, is when Tom recognizes that "for all the miles he has traveled he has never really broken the tender ties with his mother and his sister."[26] Although Tom departs in anger, with his mother calling him a "selfish dreamer" and his sister retreating into her world of glass figures, he is still connected to them.

Tom Wingfield tells us about the last contact the family had from their fleeing father. It is a postcard that reads: "Hello—Goodbye!" This sets up a theme about life's anticipations and ultimately life's limits. Scholar Judith Thompson writes that the pattern of this play is seen when one compares Amanda's wild success as a belle with many callers to Laura's one futile evening with Jim O'Connor. The play's pattern becomes "the inevitable fall of romantic aspirations to existential limitations."[27] This means that life's realities will probably overwhelm our dreams.

Poetic Imagery in Dialogue

Some critics think that the image of the Wingfields goes beyond that of a struggling single mother, a reclusive daughter, and a dreamer escapist son. Judith Thompson sees the image of this family as universal. They represent modern man's separation from God and his fellow human beings. She believes Williams uses poetic imagery in an otherwise realistic drama to make this metaphor clear.

Examples of poetic images are:

AMANDA: You did all this to deceive me, just for deception?

LAURA: Mother, when you're disappointed, you get that awful suffering look on your face, like the picture of Jesus's mother in the museum!

AMANDA: I've seen such pitiful cases in the South—barely tolerated spinsters living upon the grudging patronage of sister's husband or brother's wife—stuck away in some little mousetrap of a room—encouraged by one in-law to visit another—little birdlike women without any nest—eating the crust of humility all their life!

TOM: Man is by instinct a lover, a hunter, a fighter, and none of those instincts are given much play at the warehouse!

TOM: [about the Paradise Dance Hall] . . . a large glass sphere that hung from the ceiling. It would turn slowly about and filter the dusk with delicate rainbow colors . . . Couples would come outside . . . you could see them kissing behind ash pits and telephone poles. This was the compensation for lives that passed like mine, without any change or adventure. . . . All the world was waiting for bombardments.

TOM: [as the Narrator] The cities swept about me like dead leaves, leaves that were brightly colored but torn away from the branches. . . . I pass the lighted window of a shop where perfume is sold. The window is filled with pieces of colored glass, tiny transparent bottles in delicate colors, like bits of a shattered rainbow. Then all at once my sister touches my shoulder . . . Oh, Laura, Laura, I tried to leave you behind me, but I am more faithful than I intended to be!

Williams's theater speech draws on the natural rhythm and imagery he absorbed as a boy in Mississippi and Tennessee. He uses such devices as music, visual images projected onto screens, and special unreal lighting effects to bring his meaning to the stage.

Symbols Add to Universal Meaning

Wishing on the moon over the delicatessen symbolizes Amanda's belief in her child's romantic future, in spite of the poor, mundane life they lead. The candles and candelabra Laura uses to light her scenes are religious symbols. They came from an old church altar, and make Laura seem soft, virginal, almost angelic. Laura's glass unicorn, accidentally broken by Jim, comes from folklore. The single horn of the unicorn in medieval legend was said to heal people from poison. When Laura's unicorn's horn is broken off, we see that this reflects a special creature (like Laura) attempting to become like everyone else, which will never happen. Amanda Wingfield herself is a symbol of the lost culture of the Old South. Jim O'Connor is a symbol of the modern capitalist culture of 1945.

What Was Happening in that Menagerie?

Critics at the New York opening did not all understand or agree on what *The Glass Menagerie* meant. Robert Garland, *New York Journal-American*, February 4, 1945, wrote: "The Mother might as well be known as Fallen Grandeur. . . . Her Daughter, an unhappy moon-like cripple." Ward Morehouse, *New York Sun*, February 4, 1945, wrote: "Her daughter is the psychopathic Laura, who lives in a dream world . . . Amanda is bitter, pitiful, and ridiculous . . .". Burton Rascoe, *New York World-Telegram*, February 4, 1945, wrote:

New York Drama Critics Circle

Theater critics from all the New York City newspapers and magazines except for the New York Times, who vote on the Best Play, Best Musical, and Best Foreign Play each year on Broadway.

She was there—a simple, sanely insane, horrible Mother, pathetic and terribly human and terribly real. She succeeded in destroying every vestige of hope and beauty and joy in the lives of the two people who loved her—her son and daughter . . . she is a fluttery hen with her two soul-misshapen brood . . . she doesn't even love her son, she merely keeps him under a sense of obligation.

In spite of their diverse opinions, the critics generally agreed with Garland, when he wrote: "[T]he playwriting, which is memorable; the playacting, which is flawless; and the production, which is inimitable—makes '*The Glass Menagerie*' a masterpiece of make-believe."[28]

The Glass Menagerie won the New York Drama Critics Circle award for the best play of 1945, as well as several other monetary awards. It was a big commercial success. When Williams signed contracts with producers and publishers for this work, he granted half his royalties from it to his mother, Edwina Dakin Williams, for the rest of her life.

A RIDE ON THE STREETCAR, A SUMMER OF SMOKE

Was Blanche of "A Streetcar Named Desire" frustrated?
About as frustrated as a beast of the jungle! And Alma
Winemiller? What is frustrated about loving with such
white-hot intensity that it alters the whole direction of your
life?

—Tennessee Williams's reply to accusations he only
writes about frustrated women[1]

From his early days of poverty to his newfound prosperity, Tennessee Williams often retreated to the vibrant city of New Orleans. Although *The Glass Menagerie* made Williams a well-known playwright, people in New Orleans did not single him out. There he felt he had relative freedom from the burden of success. Williams also spent time in Acapulco, Mexico, and Key West, Florida. Wherever he moved, he hauled his portable typewriter and a trunk of manuscripts along.

During the winter of 1946, when Williams lived on Orleans Street in New Orleans, his mind was bursting with projects. He worked on a one-act play he called *Ten Blocks on the Camino Real*, which would evolve until it became a full-length production in 1953. He had also begun a play centered on a spinster's lonely life that would be called *Summer and Smoke*. Yet another story had been percolating in his mind during the

Williams works at his typewriter in 1945. By this point, he had found success with *The Glass Menagerie* and would soon solidify his position in the theater world with *A Streetcar Named Desire*.

run of *Menagerie* in New York. It involved what he called a contest between the crude sensibilities of working-class poker players and the delicacies of two Southern sisters.[2] He wrote to agent Audrey Wood that he was calling it "A Street-car Named Desire—there is one by that title that runs close by my apartment."[3]

Although Cornelius Williams regularly played poker in St. Louis hotels, his older son, Tom, had never played the game. So when he returned to Broadway for a visit, he invited men from the crew of *Menagerie* to come to his New York hotel suite and play poker. To the crew's surprise, Williams took notes on all they said and did. These poker lessons helped shape the characters of his new play.

Personal Relations Influence the Play

Williams worked on this play, along with other short stories and plays, through 1946 and into 1947. In Williams's personal life, changes occurred. Although in his mid-thirties, he had never had a long-term love relationship. During this period, a younger man named Pancho Rodriguez Gonzalez moved in with Williams. The pair moved back and forth between New Orleans and New York and summered on Nantucket Island. They were joined for the winter of 1947 in New Orleans by Reverend Walter Dakin, Williams's elderly grandfather.

At first Williams and Gonzalez had a good, balanced life together. Williams said of Pancho, "He relieved me of my greatest affliction, which is perhaps the major theme of my writings, the affliction of loneliness."[4] Yet Tennessee Williams was not able to break his habit of casual sexual affairs. Gonzalez was determined that they be faithful and committed. They fought often, sometimes physically. Once in New York, Gonzalez destroyed every piece of Williams's clothing plus his typewriter in a jealous rage. Fortunately he did not destroy the manuscripts in progress. Williams wrote in is notebook/diary: "Violence belongs to his nature as completely as it is abhorrent to mine. Most of all, I want and now must have—simple peace."[5]

During this tumultuous time with Gonzalez, Williams completed *A Streetcar Named Desire*, perhaps even using his partner's behavior for inspiration for its leading male role. Using life experiences of emotional upheaval for creating characters in his dramas became usual practice for Williams.

Streetcar opened on Broadway in December 1947 after Williams had personally auditioned Jessica Tandy in Hollywood to play Blanche. As for casting Stanley, director Elia Kazan recommended a young New York stage actor named Marlon Brando. Williams recalled that Brando drove up to Williams's rental cottage on Cape Cod. He fixed the fuses and repaired the plumbing. Brando then read for him and his director-friend Margo Jones of Dallas. Jones shouted: "This is the greatest reading I've ever heard—in or outside Texas!"[6] Brando was cast as Stanley and was forever identified with the role.

Conflicting Characters in *Streetcar*

The plot concerns the relationship between two sisters, the younger sister's husband, and the husband's best friend. What occurs between these four people is determined by their prehistory: who they were and what they did before the play begins.

The elder sister, Blanche, just over thirty, tells us gradually of her past misdeeds. The younger sister, Stella, about age twenty-six, has lived away from their family's Mississippi plantation home for many years. Much of Blanche's decline has been kept secret from Stella and Stanley Kowalski. When Blanche shows up uninvited to crash in Stella's small New

Orleans apartment, she reveals to her sister that the last members of their family have died. The plantation home has been lost to debtors, leaving Blanche homeless. Gradually we discover that Blanche has lost her job teaching high school English. Due to her affairs with various men in their hometown, Blanche is not welcome in the community and has nowhere else to turn.

Stella's prehistory is simpler. Ten years ago, the summer her father died, Stella left the family home and moved to New Orleans to find a job. She met and married Stanley Kowalski and became a housewife. In the course of the play, she also becomes a mother.

Stella says that Stanley was a master sergeant in the Engineers' Corps. Since the play opened in December 1947, we can assume that Stanley served during part of World War II. Now a salesman of machinery, witty and shrewd, Stanley's competitive nature is seen as he plays poker with male friends. He can be violent when drunk, crude and domineering. Still, Stanley demonstrates a passionate devotion to Stella and the child she will bear.

Harold "Mitch" Mitchell is Stan's best friend, coworker at the company, and fellow veteran. He also has a history of being a caregiver to his sick mother. Stella likes and respects him and feels he might be a prospective husband for Blanche. Although Mitch is more sensitive than Stanley, he is a hard, demanding man when it comes to purity in a woman.

Sexual Attraction, Fascinating Females: Stella Acts As the Pivot

The plot of *Streetcar* turns on Stella Kowalski. She is manipulated back and forth between her sister's demands that she leave what Blanche terms her brutish husband, and her husband's growing fury that Blanche is ruining their tightly balanced marriage. A loving sister, Stella tries to find a solution for Blanche's desperate position. Yet she cannot give up her sexual fulfillment with Stanley. He is also the father and supporter of her baby. It is Stella's decision not to believe that Stanley has forced himself on Blanche that allows the play to end as it does.

Scholar Louise Blackwell studied the "predicament of women" in Williams's plays. She claims all his major females "suffer from physical or emotional mutilation."[7] In the 1940s, authors rarely wrote honestly about the abuse women sometimes suffered in relationships. In the case of *Streetcar*, Blackwell notes that Blanche's prehistory includes a family of degenerates. The DuBoises gave Blanche high-class airs, culture, and education. Still, they were weaklings who wasted her land and passed on no moral strength. The Kowalskis learned how to fight for survival. They were Polish immigrants who endured hard times, often producing dominant males like Stanley. When Stanley's masculine power collides with Blanche's sexual past and superior attitude, an explosion is bound to occur. Blanche's downfall becomes inevitable.

Symbols Are Woven Through Characters and Objects

Critics have said that Blanche can be a symbol for many things. Chris Jones, writing for the Roundabout Theatre Company Magazine, said: "Blanche . . . is a metaphor for lost souls . . . and a reminder that so-called social progress almost always has its victims."[8] Edward Hall, director of a recent New York production, said Blanche was the kind of genteel, emotionally damaged woman that had no place in postwar America. "She's quite literally at the end of the line right from when we first meet her."[9]

Marlon Brando, Kim Taylor, and Jessica Tandy star in the 1947 Broadway production of *A Streetcar Named Desire*.

Stanley may be a metaphor for the new middle-class, self-made workingman. Blanche, however, calls him an animal in scene 4: "There's even something sub-human—something not quite to the stage of humanity yet. Yes, something ape-like about him."[10] She begs Stella to leave him and not hang back with the brutes. Stella, refusing to see this image of her husband, embraces him as soon as he returns. Later, Blanche tells Mitch, "The first time I laid eyes on him, I thought to myself, that man is my executioner. That man will destroy me."[11]

Blanche does things that symbolize how she truly sees herself. She obsessively bathes. This is because she knows that she is not clean or pure inside. Blanche keeps the lights low with colored paper lanterns on them. This allows her to keep up an illusion of gentility and youthful beauty. She tells Stella: "When people are soft—soft people have got to shimmer and glow—they've got to put on soft colors, the colors of butterfly wings, and put a—a paper lantern over the light. . . . I'm fading now. I don't know how much longer I can turn the trick."[12] The image of the fading butterfly, flittering and falling, gives us a preview of how Blanche will fail at the end of the play.

Williams uses the poker game as a metaphor to reflect life in the Kowalski apartment. Judith J. Thompson writes of the game: "Stanley's fluctuating fortunes at cards reflect his changing status in the existential game of survival played between him and Blanche."[13] Stanley, a fierce card player and bitter loser, figures out what the real cards are in Blanche's hand. Although Blanche almost finds her savior in fellow player Mitch, Stanley makes sure she ends up out of the game and out of his life forever.

In scene 8 of the play, Blanche uses candles and their light as a metaphor for purity and inner beauty. When Mitch deserts her birthday party, she asks Stella to save the candles for her baby's birthdays: "I hope the candles are going to glow in his life and I hope that his eyes are going to be like candles, like two blue candles lighted in a white cake!"[14] This echoes a similar metaphor of Laura's candles in *Glass Menagerie*.

Just as he did in *Menagerie*, Tennessee Williams wrote directions for the staging, sets, lighting, and musical background of this play. The eleven scenes are like scenes in a film, with sudden starts of the action and dynamic conclusions. The author's directions for lighting and sound effects, including musical underscoring, make *Streetcar* a total experience for the audience. The sounds of blues and jazz, which fill the real French Quarter in New Orleans, help create a heightened sensual feel, like a film's underscoring. These sounds key the audience into changes in emotional content that are coming. Low, moody lights in the apartment, ominous flashes of lightning, the moment when Mitch rips off a colored paper lantern and holds Blanche's face under the naked bulb are examples of cinematic style. These are ways to focus our vision on characters and force our response, similar to camera shots and lighting effects in cinema.

Forcing the Issue of Sexual Violence

Williams stopped writing about broad socialist issues as he did in his first plays. However, he was the first playwright on the American stage to deal openly with the crime of sexual assault. Of course, the act is not visualized, as Stanley forces Blanche onto his bed and the lights go out. Still, it was a shocking moment to see and hear on stage. Critic Kimball King notes that although Blanche has had many sexual affairs, Stanley's assault of her is "nonetheless a rape, a crime of violence rather than simply a sexual act; we witness Blanche DuBois's destruction by Kowalski."[15]

Streetcar Gives the Critics Quite a Trip

On its Broadway opening, December 4, 1947, critic Ward Morehouse wrote for the *New York Sun*: "*A Streetcar Named Desire* is not a play for the squeamish. It is often coarse and harrowing . . . but it is a playwriting job of enormous gusto and vitality and poignance."

Williams Hawkins wrote for the *New York World-Telegram*: "Williams models out of the rawest materials and his finished art is harsh realism. It is lost souls that preoccupy him." Hawkins recognizes that the play is an account of the conflict between Blanche and Stanley: "[T]he one thing they know in common is physical desire." Stanley, open and honest, likes to eat and drink and make love whenever he wants. Blanche must rationalize everything she does. Hawkins sees "the two essential planes of the character" in Blanche—and notes "There are scenes of violence and raw emotion that leave you gasping."

Louis Kronenberger wrote in *New York PM* that the play is the best of the season, "the one that reveals the most talent, the one that attempts the most truth." He sees Blanche as a "demonically driven kind of liar—the one who lies to the world because she must lie to herself." Kronenberger said the middle of the play was too static and repetitious, but the final third with its genuine release of emotional excitement, with the conflict between Blanche and Stanley, "is quite often good drama!"[16]

The play's finale is as moving as any scene in contemporary theater. Stanley has Blanche committed to a mental institution. When the institution's doctor and matron come for Blanche, both Stella and Mitch break down in tears of guilt and regret.

To keep leading their lives, Stella as Stanley's wife and mother of his child, and Mitch as Stanley's best friend, they step aside and let Stanley get rid of Blanche. At the final moment, we can only hope that treatment will give Blanche some kind of future. As Blanche clings to the doctor, she exits, saying: "Whoever you are—I have always depended on the kindness of strangers."

Goodbye Pancho, Hello Frank: Williams's Private Life Changes

Life with Tennessee Williams involved his constant writing, traveling, drinking, cigarette smoking, and strange friendships. Williams, although basically a strong man, still had health issues. He had many surgeries on reoccurring cataracts on his eyes, plus intestinal problems. Anyone who lived with Williams would have to understand his high-strung nerves and obsession with illness. He found such a man in 1948, ten years his junior. He was a Sicilian American from New Jersey named Frank Merlo. Williams wrote about it in his *Memoirs*, saying that "it was clear to me that my heart, too long accustomed to transitory attachments, had found in the young Sicilian a home at last."[17]

Dakin Williams, knowing that his brother was obsessively drawn to casual sex partners who could be dangerous, called Frank the best person in his life. "My brother left every practical detail of his life to Frank, and he discharged everything wonderfully well. He cared for Grandfather . . . Frank was a unique man."[18] Close friends Paul Bigelow and Christopher Isherwood stated that Frank Merlo tried to give order and stability to Williams's nomadic life. Maria St. Just, a Russian actress and dancer who became Williams's great friend, said after meeting Frank in 1948 that he truly loved Tennessee

Williams for what he was. "He had great integrity and great dignity."[19] Unfortunately, Frank Merlo, like Pancho, also wanted monogamy, which Tennessee was unable to maintain. Hurt, Frank decided the only release for his own pride was to have a few casual sex partners himself. Nevertheless, Tennessee and "Frankie" still loved each other for the rest of Frank's life.

Summer and Smoke Blows Hot and Cold

Not every play produced by Tennessee Williams was an instant smash hit. *Summer and Smoke* opened on Broadway on October 6, 1948, and ran only three months. Some critics called it pretentious, boring, too long, and too dependent on emotions. Only Brooks Atkinson of the *New York Times* saw its beauty, poetry, and artistry. Williams wrote to his friend Donald Windham about his feelings regarding *Summer and Smoke*'s production on October 19, 1948: "I'm afraid Margo [Jones, the director] did a rather mediocre job. Not inspired, not vital as [Elia] Kazan would have been and as the play so dreadfully needed . . . I am not depressed or unhappy about it, but I regret it was not converted into the exciting theatre that the best direction could have made it."[20]

Elia Kazan was the director who took on *Streetcar Named Desire* and made it rise on the heat of passion and fly on the wings of feeling. Williams knew he could not always depend on landing the very popular Kazan or an equally sensitive director. After its modest run on Broadway, *Summer and Smoke* was revived. Four years later on April 24, 1952, it opened at the Circle in the Square, a repertory company in New York's Greenwich Village. This version starring young Geraldine Page was a solid hit. Because it was a major work playing in a theater downtown, people began calling it off-Broadway theater.

Williams planned to explore the theme of the "good woman" versus the "fallen woman" in *Summer and Smoke*. He felt that American morality clung to the Victorian ideal that to be a good woman, one must be pure before marriage and faithful to one's spouse after marriage. A woman who gives in to lust and passion outside of marriage is considered a fallen woman. In order to define this contrast in moral behavior, Williams set *Summer and Smoke* back in time to the Victorian era in a small town in the American South.

Alma Winemiller, the repressed minister's daughter in *Summer and Smoke*, is portrayed as a good woman. We also meet Rosa Gonzales, who gives herself to young Dr. John Buchanan in the hopes of improving her lot in life and because she is open to enjoying sex outside marriage. As for Dr. Buchanan himself, as a rakish bachelor and professional icon in town, he seems above moral criticism.

The Role of Religion: The Battle of Body vs. Soul.

Alma Winemiller is seemingly inspired by the young Edwina Dakin, the repressed daughter of her Protestant minister father. Williams, his sister Rose, and his brother Dakin, all felt the heavy hand of guilt laid upon them by their uptight mother if they showed any inclination to try sexual relation-ships outside of marriage. Obviously Tennessee could not marry, as homosexual men could not have legal partnerships during his lifetime. Rose was mentally and emotionally unable to be a wife. Only Dakin managed to wed in his late thirties and have a "legitimate" physical relationship. But Tennessee openly explored the difficulty and injustice of life for the

Almas of the world who were taught to deny the needs of the flesh, with what he hoped was tenderness and sympathy.

The *Smoke* of a Burning Heart

Williams lays out the stage carefully for *Summer and Smoke.* In the center is the town fountain. It contains the statue of an angel with the inscription "Eternity." On one side is the Episcopal rectory. On the other side is Doctor Buchanan's home and medical office. Alma's father, Reverend Winemiller, treats the spirit. John Buchanan and his father treat the body. The angel in between pours forth pure healing water and hope.

Although we meet Alma and John briefly when they are adolescents in the Prologue, the play presents them in their twenties. Alma speaks and acts as if she were much older. She had to replace her mother as the "wife" of the Rectory because her mother is emotionally disturbed. Alma has always been attracted to John. Yet she tends to put men off by being too nervous, judgmental, and repressed.

John is drawn to Alma but cannot relate to her. His need for physical satisfaction is met by Rosa Gonzalez, the daughter of the owner of the Moon Lake Casino. Critic Thomas P. Adler says that Alma and John constantly misread each other. "Neither one knows until very late in the play what it means to be a fully integrated human being."[21]

Balance between natural sexual attraction and good moral conduct is difficult for Alma and John to achieve. They have many gifts but seem to squander them in their search for self-identity. Alma tells John that love is not just coupling: "[T]here are some women, John, who can bring their hearts to it, also—who can bring their souls to it!"[22] John replies by giving Alma an anatomy lesson. He explains the brain is hungry for truth, the belly needs nourishment, and the sex part is hungry for love. "You've fed none—nothing. Love or truth . . . nothing but hand-me-down notions."[23]

Summer and Smoke Has Symbolic Meaning

The play's title refers to the long hot summer in Alma's life during which she kept herself chaste despite her love for John. Smoke results from a low, smoldering fire. Alma tells John: "[T]he girl who said 'no' doesn't exist any more, she died last

Williams works with director Margo Jones on the 1948 stage production of *Summer and Smoke*. The play had a disapointing run but enjoyed several successful revivals in later years.

summer—suffocated in smoke from something on fire inside her."[24] The slow burn of Alma's growing sexuality is symbolized by the smoke.

Later, Alma confesses to Doctor John that she has been so disoriented and repressed that she thought she was dying. "But now the Gulf wind has blown that feeling away, like a cloud of smoke."[25] She yearns to love John with body and spirit. For John, their love is too late. He has put his image of Alma back up on the pedestal, like the angel's statue, and given his pledge to the younger, passionate but innocent Nellie.

Alma must swallow her rejection and frustration and act upon her newly recognized sexuality. At the play's end, Alma is determined to try having relationships with men. She accepts a date with a man for the Moon Lake Casino, saluting the angel as she leaves.

The *New York Times* critic Brooks Atkinson said about the playwright in his review: "The twin themes of his tone poem are clearly stated: spirit and flesh, order and anarchy. He has caught them in the troubled brooding of two human hearts."[26]

Williams the Revisionist: How *Smoke* Became *Nightingale*

Williams was still not satisfied with this work, so he tried rewriting *Summer and Smoke*. This revision was copyrighted in 1964 as *The Eccentricities of a Nightingale*. Both plays are set in Glorious Hill, Mississippi, between 1900 and 1916 and have many of the same characters.

Williams said about *Nightingale* that is was a "substantially different play from *Summer and Smoke*, and I prefer it. It is less conventional and melodramatic . . . I hope that its publication may lead to its production . . . and may confirm my feeling that it is a better work than the play from which it derived."[27]

In order to see Williams's obsessive striving for perfection, something he set out to do from his days as a university student-playwright, we need to make a comparison between *Smoke* and *Nightingale*. Why did Williams call them substantially different? And why was *Nightingale* superior?

The first obvious difference is that the author deleted some important secondary roles, such as John and Alma as children; John's father, the senior Dr. Buchanan; Rosa Gonzales and her father Papa Gonzales, the owners of the Casino; Nellie Ewell, the young woman who ends up engaged to John; Mr. Kramer; and Dusty. The roles of Alma and John's mothers are amplified. Williams set up *Nightingale* as a three-act play with a total of nine scenes, whereas *Smoke* had been a two-act play with a total of twelve scenes. Since *Nightingale* runs about thirty-seven pages shorter than *Smoke*, it is a tighter, more focused play.

Although it would not matter to a theater audience, Williams gave each of *Nightingale*'s acts a special title: Act 1 is "The Feeling of a Singer," act 2 is "The Tenderness of a Mother," and act 3 is "A Cavalier's Plume." The titles do have meanings. The first act's title implies that the excess of emotion we see in "'singer" Alma is a cause of her becoming one of the avoided "eccentrics" of the town. The second act's title is a bitter irony, since the mothers of Alma and John have become more imperative characters who are damaging the lives of their children. And the third act's title uses the image taken from one of Alma and John's favorite poems, in which a man dreams of becoming a dashing cavalier. But the plume is really upon Alma's hat. She thinks it may represent the beautiful, desirable woman that she will never be. John tells her: "I think your honesty is the plume on your hat. And you ought to wear it proudly." Alma finds the strength to reply: "Proudly or not, I shall wear it."[28] In a small cold hotel room with a miraculously burning fireplace, they spend the night together.

While John may be a more steady and dependent, less dashing and reckless character in *Nightingale*, Alma has become more deeply realized. When Alma decides that one day and night with John, the boy she has always loved, will be worth any sacrifice and eventual loneliness it may bring her, she is taking charge of her neuroses, even her own fate.

Time passes. When Alma appears in a brief Epilogue with a young traveling salesman, she admits that no one asks her to sing anymore, then gives him a brief history of Glorious Hill. Home of the county courthouse, where slaves were once sold, and the Episcopal church where her father was rector before his death, as well as the fountain, with the angel titled "Eternity," Alma seems the proud tour guide. Unlike Alma at the end of

> **irony**
>
> The incongruity of an expected situation (or its outcome) and the actual situation (or its outcome). In language, irony is the deliberate use of words to contrast an apparent meaning with the words' intended meaning (which are usually the complete opposite of each other).

Smoke, she does not require tranquilizers to get through the evening.

Then she asks the salesman if he'd like to see a district called "Tiger Town," which can afford the pleasures of saloons, arcades, and rooms for rent. Nervously, the young man agrees. Since there seems to be no one left in Alma's life to boss her or condemn her she decides she will take her comforts when she can. She tells the salesman gaily: "I'm not going to lose you, before I've lost you."[29]

Williams's instincts were good in his reshaping of *Smoke* into *Nightingale*. This version of the work succeeded on

Broadway in 1971. However, both versions are available and often receive revivals.

When asked later to reflect on his heroines, Williams said: "I think the character I like most is Miss Alma. She is my favorite because I came out so late [sexually] and so did Alma . . . Miss Alma grew up in the shadow of the rectory, and so did I."[30] Critics agree that there are personality traits of Tom Williams in Alma, as well as some from his mother and sister, Edwina and Rose.

Tennessee's brother Dakin Williams, who became a lawyer after serving in the military, drew up a trust for their sister Rose. It gave her half the royalties from her brother's play *Summer and Smoke,* and its later version, *Eccentricities of a Nightingale.* This permitted Rose to pay for superior residential and mental health care. Williams was proud to have helped his mother and his sister have as much freedom in their lives as money could buy.

THE SHOCKING DUALITY OF THE SINGLE HEART: EXAMINING CAT ON A HOT TIN ROOF

Both versions [of Cat] will be published, and confidentially I still much prefer the original. It was harder and purer: a blacker play but one that cut closer to the bone of truth.

—Tennessee Williams to critic Brooks Atkinson[1]

With the playwright's help, Tennessee Williams's family members were now able to move on with their lives. Thanks to her gift of theater royalties, Williams's mother Edwina decided to divorce her husband and live independently in St. Louis. Rose Williams spent most of her time in mental institutions in Farmington, Missouri, and upstate New York.

Williams's restless nature drove him, along with Frank Merlo, and sometimes with author friends Gore Vidal and Truman Capote, to tour Europe throughout 1949 and 1950. That winter, with Frank and Grandfather Dakin in Key West, Williams produced the first draft of *The Rose Tattoo*. He dedicated the play to Merlo, whose Sicilian family inspired it. This play will be criticized in the next chapter.

Biographer Ronald Hayman notes that from this time period on, Williams took up a dangerous habit. He had started

Williams stands in front of his studio in Key West, Florida. He enjoyed the relaxed atmosphere of the area and was able to maintain a fairly low profile in his daily life.

KEY WEST: A WRITER'S HAVEN

Williams first fell for Key West in 1941 and visited regularly until he bought his home there on Duncan Street in 1949. Other literary stars who lived for a time on the Key were Ernest Hemingway; poets Robert Frost, Elizabeth Bishop, James Merrill, John Ciardi, and Richard Wilbur; and novelists Philip Caputo, James Leo Herlihy, Thomas McGuane, Ralph Ellison, and John Hershey. Each January the Key West Literary Seminar celebrates this rich literary heritage.

"experimenting with pills—phenobarbital and secobarbital" in 1949.[2] Williams wrote to a longtime friend from New York, Donald Windham, about his life in Key West in December 1949: "[M]y ratio of concerns is something like this: 50% work and worry over work, 35% the perpetual struggle against lunacy . . . 15% a very true and very tender love for those who have been and are close to me as friends and as lover."[3] At the time, his obsession with work was growing to 89 percent. His anxiety and fear of illness was just as high as ever.

In the early 1950s, Williams combined alcohol with regular use of pills, primarily to sleep. Friends noted that he sometimes took Seconal (a barbiturate prescribed for insomnia) with a whiskey chaser, a destructive practice. He continued to rewrite *Camino Real*, now a full-length play made up of journeying and surreal scenes. In spite of taking alcohol with prescription drugs, Williams finished his next major play, *Cat on a Hot Tin Roof*, in 1953.

During the 1950s, Tennessee Williams wrote about two difficult subjects that were seldom mentioned on the American stage: homosexuality and cancer. Being open about one's sexual orientation at this time was difficult. Williams never

69

hid his gay life. However, he doubted that the public was ready to explore the subject in his plays. Incurable illness and a crude, overbearing father figure were also subjects that might put off an audience.

A play about a prep-school boy struggling with being gay opened on Broadway in 1953. *Tea and Sympathy* by Robert Anderson received a good reception. Williams, encouraged, finished *Cat on a Hot Tin Roof* and gave it to his agent.

Williams did obscure the nature of the love that the hero Brick felt for his dead friend Skipper. In an interview for *Theatre Arts* magazine in July 1955, Williams stated: "Brick is definitely not a homosexual . . . Brick's self pity and recourse to the bottle are not the result of a guilty conscience in that regard."[4] Williams said that Brick's bitterness about the tragedy of Skipper's death was what made him drink, "although I do suggest that at least at some time in his life, there have been unrealized abnormal tendencies."[5]

Cat on a Hot Tin Roof opened in New York in March 1955. It won both the New York Drama Critics Circle Award and the Pulitzer Prize. Yet Williams was not satisfied. Twenty years later, the times were right for a revision of this play. It is this final version that further defines the characters. The 1974–1975 Broadway revival script is the one most commonly produced today.

A Birthday Party Gone Bad

The plot of *Cat* spans the time of a birthday party on the expansive Pollitt plantation in the Mississippi Delta. Big Daddy Pollitt is turning sixty-five. His wife, Ida (called Big Mama), his elder son, Gooper, and his wife, Mae, plus their five small children and assorted friends and servants, throw him a celebration. The action never leaves the bedroom of

Brick Pollitt, the younger son, and his wife, Margaret, called Maggie. Signs of the celebration are seen off an open gallery and heard from offstage.

The action is driven by the goals of the three main characters. Brick's goal is to drown his present pain in alcohol. Maggie's goal is to win back her husband's love and sexual attention, as well as to secure his inheritance. Big Daddy's goal is to beat cancer, then spend the rest of his life as tyrannical master of his vast holdings.

The three secondary characters have their goals as well. Brother Gooper, a Memphis lawyer, and Mae, his grasping wife, are determined the Pollitt plantation should be theirs to run after Big Daddy dies. Ida Pollitt's main goal is to keep her husband alive, even though on most levels he rejects her. She also wants to keep the plantation in her own hands.

These six characters clash over and over throughout the course of the birthday party. At Blanche's birthday party in *Streetcar Named Desire*, the one invited guest fails to show up. This time, far too many guests arrive to win the favor of Big Daddy Pollitt.

The major characters must search for painful truths about who they really are. Longtime communication barriers between Brick and his wife, and Brick and his father, must be broken down. Williams describes their coming together as "a thundercloud of a common crisis."[6]

As summer lightning and rumbling thunder threaten outside the house, explosive storms take place within.

The Impact of Ghosts

The play deals with three ghosts, spirits of dead friends that impact Brick, Maggie, and Big Daddy. Skipper was Brick's best friend and football teammate. His love for Brick and his death after Brick's desertion make him a character that still influences this story. Skipper not only haunts Brick, but also Maggie, who slept with him so he might "prove" he did not desire Brick physically. Her guilty act helped destroy him.

Two other ghosts, Jack Straw and Peter Uchello, were the farmers who gave Big Daddy his start on the plantation. They were also a homosexual couple that shared a bed in the same room now used by Brick and Maggie. Big Daddy understood these men. He tells Brick: "When Jack Straw died, why old Peter Uchello quit eatin' like a dog does when its master's dead, and died too."[7] Is it possible the ghosts of Straw and Uchello reflect the relationship of Brick and Skipper? Williams says Brick explodes as if "a quiet mountain blew suddenly up in volcanic flame," and accuses his father of asking if he and Skipper "did—sodomy—together?"[8] Brick's strong denial is accepted by Big Daddy.

During the last act, Big Daddy faces his favored son's misery over his lost glory and guilt about loving but failing Skipper. Brick then tells his father that they have hidden the truth from him. Big Daddy has inoperable cancer, and he will die soon. Brick must still grapple with his alcoholism, guilt, and crisis of self-identity. Maggie takes charge at the play's finale. She bitterly fights with Gooper and Mae, defending Brick's right to the estate. Her strength and female determination to draw Brick back and conceive his child make her the triumphant survivor in the end.

Williams once said that he heard the expression "nervous as a cat on a hot tin roof" from his father. This colorful picture was a good image for Margaret Pollitt. She reflects the powerful life force of the cat.

Ben Gazzara and Barbara Bel Geddes act out a scene between
Brick and Margaret in the 1955 Broadway production of *Cat on a
Hot Tin Roof*.

Strong Original Characters

Maggie is a beautiful young woman with a strong need for love and financial and social security. Although Southern women of the mid-twentieth century were expected to be gentle and retiring, Maggie cannot behave that way. Maggie admits that she has been forced to undergo "this hideous transformation, become—hard! Frantic!—cruel! . . . I can't afford to be thin-skinned anymore."[9] Maggie will not let Brick throw away his inheritance. She was "born poor, raised poor," and believes it is impossible to grow old with no money. She bluntly tells Brick that there are family members who want to cut them out because "you drink and I've borne no children."[10] Critic Dianne Cafagna says of her: "Maggie, like cancer, is the harsh reality the Pollitt family must learn to live with."[11]

Maggie has been trying to seduce her own husband because Brick clings to his drinking instead of his wife. Her beauty attracts other men, she tells Brick. Yet she wants no one but him. Claiming he is unnaturally attached to his late friend, she cries: "Skipper is dead! I'm alive. Maggie the cat is alive!"[12]

Throughout the play, Brick reveals his prehistory. He was a handsome, talented football quarterback at the University of Mississippi. There he fell in love with Maggie and grew deeply involved with teammate Skipper. Not able to give up their glory days on the field, Brick and Skipper joined with others to form a semiprofessional team. Brick recalls keeping up "the aerial attack that made us famous."[13]

After Brick suffers an injury and can no longer play, Skipper falls apart without him. Brick tries sports announcing, but his depression and alcoholism keep him from being a success. He retreats to his parents' home, where he is forced to fend off his wife, his brother, and his father. Saying he "hates mendacity," or untruthfulness, Brick finally must spit out the truth of his refusing Skipper's love for him. His lack of courage and self-knowledge made Skipper slide into alcoholism and suicide.

Big Daddy Pollitt is an unusual character in American literature. He is a self-made man who had to quit school at ten and work doggedly until he became overseer for Straw and Uchello. Usually such self-made men are admirable. Big Daddy is coarse, proud, vulgar, blunt, and self-centered. We meet him when he has been facing cancer, which in the 1950s was almost always fatal. A false report is given him on his birthday that claims he has no more than a spastic colon. However, everyone but he and his wife knows the truth. A fresh lease on life causes him to reach out to Brick, the one person in his life he actually cares for. During this process, he cruelly rejects his wife and older son.

Big Daddy does possess honesty and emotional courage. He is willing to go the distance with Brick to get to the bottom of his drinking and despair. Once Brick blurts out the truth of his malignant cancer, Big Daddy finds the strength to face his own death.

Each of these characters leads what Williams thought of as tortured inner lives. Both Maggie and Big Mama are women who can love openly and endure the slights they get from their men. The love experienced by these three married couples is revealed to be quite different. A father's varying love for sons who are distant and even threatening to him is explored. The deep and forbidden love Skipper felt for Brick is brought out into the open. The difference between sexual attraction, need, and pure affection is painfully portrayed.

A Family Filled With Mendacity

There are no inner monologues in *Cat*, as in previous Williams plays. These characters verbally blast each other out loud. They demand truth. Big Daddy does not care if his truth telling hurts people. However, others lie for various reasons. Gooper and Mae lie to Big Daddy about his cancer so they can get through his birthday and court his favor. Maggie lies to Big Daddy about being pregnant, because she badly wants the lie to become truth. Saddest of all is Brick's lying to himself. He was unable to accept the unquestioning love he got from Skipper. Now he admits that he knew Skipper loved him—but he denied Skipper to the end.

Both Big Daddy and Brick, when told by their wives at separate times that they really love them, say "wouldn't it be funny if it were true?" Williams shows us men who have never been able to fully love and who are unable to accept unconditional love in return. The Pollitt family, like the Wingfield family in *The Glass Menagerie*, are universal. Although they love one another, they also deceive, deny, and hide feelings from one another. In the end, they do the best they can to go on.

A final theme in *Cat* is an exploration of the role of money and power. Williams knew wealthy plantation owners in Mississippi. He wrote *Cat* after he himself earned his way out of poverty and was financially secure. He realized that like Big Daddy Pollitt, people often used their money and power to buy attention and affection. He also knew, as Maggie Pollitt says, that it is not so terrible to be poor when you are young and beautiful. Yet when you get older, Williams indicates poverty becomes impossible to bear.

Williams (*left*) accepts the Drama Critics' Circle Best Play award for *Cat on a Hot Tin Roof* in 1955. Presenting the award is theater critic Walter Kerr.

Critics Howl for Cat

Walter Kerr, writing for the *New York Herald Tribune*, called *Cat on a Hot Tin Roof* "a beautifully written, perfectly directed, stunningly acted play of evasions."[14] He wrote that in spite of every major character's search for truth, the play ends by evading it.

Brooks Atkinson, writing for the *New York Times*, said one of the play's "great achievements is the honesty and simplicity of the craftsmanship. It seems not to have been written. It is . . . the basic truth . . . it is not only part of the truth of life: it is the absolute truth of the theatre."[15] Yet Atkinson recognizes the evasions of the play. He said of the main characters: "[L]ies are the only refuge they have from the ugly truths that possess their minds."[16]

Not every critic admired the play's veracity or appreciated the frankness of the characters. Robert Coleman from the *New York Daily Mirror* said that "much of the language is right from the barnyard . . . but these people are anything but aristocrats and much less than decent. They are neurotic, frustrated, and fascinated by bawdy speech."[17] Coleman felt the characters were "disturbed and disturbing people, tired of living and scared of dying."[18] The actors were praised for generating real emotion and excitement and the author recognized for creating almost operatic monologues and dialogues.

Once again, Williams was not sure which version of this play would survive, considering the second version of the ending looked with more painful honesty at Brick's bisexual relationships with both Maggie and Skipper. As time went by and the public understanding of bisexuality become more widespread, the second ending was performed.

When the play had revivals on Broadway in 1975, in London in 2001, and in New York in 2003–2004, critics assessed the revised script and liked it. As London critic Lizzie Loveridge said in 2001, "The near half century has seen attitude changes towards gender but this play still works. Families still battle over inheritance. Sexually dysfunctional marriages still exist. Men and women still abuse each other. This production . . . deserves to be a highlight of the London theatrical year."[19]

RESTLESS ROAMING IN THE FIFTIES: SELF DECEPTION IN THE ROSE TATTOO AND THE NIGHT OF THE IGUANA

The Night of the Iguana is a play whose theme is how to live beyond despair and still live . . . I despair of love being lasting and of people getting along together . . . as nations and as individuals.

—Tennessee Williams, at the time he composed *The Night of the Iguana*, 1962[1]

Before *Cat on a Hot Tin Roof*, Tennessee Williams wrote a tribute to a fictional community of Sicilian Americans on the Gulf Coast near New Orleans. While *The Rose Tattoo* was not based on a true family history, the play reflected experiences Williams had enjoyed with his partner Frank Merlo and the Merlo family in New Jersey, and during trips to Sicily. It was produced on Broadway in 1950 and was a resounding success.

No matter what his health issues or emotional upheavals, Williams never let a year go by that he did not produce a script. Besides *Cat on a Hot Tin Roof*, he wrote nine other plays in the decade of the 1950s. Four of them have become enduring

Williams is seen here in New York City in 1961, a year after *The Night of the Iguana* opened on Broadway.

parts of his canon and will be discussed later. By the end of the decade, tired and starting to doubt his ability to write another major hit play, Williams produced *The Night of the Iguana*. This richly layered study of American tourists and expatriates took place in the steamy summer of 1940, located in the fictional Mexican resort town of Puerto Barrio. A Broadway production opened in 1960.

Rose and *Iguana* are probably considered the most important of Williams' work after *The Glass Menagerie, A Streetcar Named Desire*, and *Cat on a Hot Tin Roof*. Although these plays were not the incredible money-makers that the first three were, they show a broad artistic vision and tenderness of spirit, and have remained popular. Each became an honored film, from which Williams derived much of his profit.

canon

The complete list of books by any author regarded as authentically his work.

The Glass Menagerie and *A Streetcar Named Desire* were Williams's first plays to land lucrative Hollywood contracts. Theater companies around the world were producing them. Tennessee Williams became a rich playwright by age thirty-nine. His lifestyle had become one of restless roaming, from writing retreats in the South to rehearsal halls in the North. His holidays were usually spent in southern Europe. The only real estate Williams owned was his simple home on Duncan Street in Key West, Florida.

In 1950, Williams published his only novel, *The Roman Spring of Mrs. Stone*, about the emotional breakdown of an American widow who falls for a Roman gigolo. Mrs. Stone in many ways reflects the troubles visited on Williams himself, as the stress of life as a celebrity playwright took its toll.

Common Themes in *Tattoo* and *Iguana*

Serefina della Rosa of *The Rose Tattoo*, the bride who during her fifteen-year marriage gave herself faithfully to her husband, is a good woman. Hannah Jelkes, the unwed painter who devoted her life to art and to caring for her grandfather in *The Night of the Iguana*, is a good woman. Serefina and Hannah have held their needs and passions in check. However, each of these strong female characters is special. They live in different times and cultures, and have unique personalities and gifts.

Rose and *Iguana* also both feature a fallen woman who embraces sex outside of marriage. We meet Estelle in *The Rose Tattoo*, and later hear her admit she had an affair with Serefina's husband. Maxine in *The Night of the Iguana* is a major character, lusty and recently widowed. Maxine contents herself with casual sex with the boys who work for her. If Reverend Lawrence Shannon will be her lover, she will take in the fallen cleric.

The second common theme is the role of religion in a relationship. Serefina and Hannah are believers in God. Serefina is childlike in her faith, a follower of the Catholic Church and its Holy Virgin Mary, about whom she says: "She gives me signs."[2] Also, she is deeply superstitious. Hannah searches for God in art, nature, people, even her grandfather's poem. However, the men that these women desire have strayed from their moral code. They are fighting a battle between body and soul. Each play studies how the need for these men affects these women in their beliefs.

Finally, Williams considers the decline of innocence as people head toward the end of their life. Purity gives way to corruption. Williams wrote in one of his last plays (*Something Cloudy, Something Clear*, 1981) a verse on this subject.

His character August says: "God give me death before thirty, before my clean heart has grown dirty, soiled with the dust of much living, more wanting and taking than giving."[3] Serefina discovers her adored husband, Rosario, is not only a smuggler—he has also cheated on her. Hannah's friend Reverend Shannon is near suicide due to the demise of his personal honor and faith. How these women react to these situations makes for great drama.

Scholar Nancy Tischler makes a point about Tennessee Williams and his use of blending romance and passion. She says: "He wandered through life and wove colorful romantic pictures onto the dark background of his increasing realism . . . he lived as a peripatetic poet, one of the everlasting company of fugitives who discover their vocation in their art."[4]

Passion, Pain, and Comedy Blend in *Rose Tattoo*

In *The Rose Tattoo*, Williams chose a potentially serious subject, the devastating loss of a beloved husband and the problem of raising a teenage daughter alone. However, his treatment is warm, folksy, wildly emotional, and often comic. The success of the play depends on the audience believing in the widowed seamstress Serefina Delle Rosa and her reactions to her life. At the play's beginning Serefina awaits her beloved trucker husband Rosario, who is winding up a smuggling run. After he is killed making the run, Serefina clings to her grieving widow's role for three years. As her lovely daughter Rosa graduates from high school at age fifteen [which must indicate she was a very advanced student] and falls for the seemingly honorable Jack, Serefina must realign her role as a protective mother, a Sicilian community member, and perhaps in the future, the wife of another man.

Serefina's Sicilian friends and her new suitor, the sexy, warm, and playful Alvaro, must also be believable. Often the characters seem childlike, impulsive, and unnatural to a mid-twentieth-century audience. Sicilian customs, while portrayed with accuracy by Williams, can appear to be quite foreign.

When Serefina first meets Jack, she informs him: "We don't leave the girls with the boys they're not engaged to."[5] When Jack replies, "Mrs. Delle Rosa, this is the United States," she reminds him: "But we are Sicilians and we are not cold blooded." Serefina makes Jack swear to the Virgin Mary that he will respect Rosa's virginity. Williams admitted that his people in *Rose Tattoo* were acting on instinct, not always on reason.

As critic Brooks Atkinson commented, "[T]hose gusty and volatile Sicilians blow hot and cold at bewildering speed."[6] Atkinson also recognized that Serefina makes the entire play work, as she "speaks the autobiography of her soul."[7]

The voices of the Sicilian community include Father DeLeo the priest, Assunta the local herbal-medic, the neighbor Strega [*strega* can mean 'witch' in Italian] and a trio of gossipy women and their raucous children. They keep Serefina grounded as she endures the hard discovery of Rosario's murder due to smuggling, and eventually, the truth of his adultery.

Serefina's painful struggle to return to her physical and emotional life is obvious to her priest, Father DeLeo, who encourages her: "You are still a young woman. Eligible for loving—and bearing again."[8] Serefina's resolution to allow both her daughter and herself to move on into life's next phase makes for a triumphant ending to this warm human drama. By accepting Alvaro's affection, Serefina starts back on the road to reclaiming her warmth and womanhood.

The roles of Serefina and Jack are played by Maureen Stapleton and Don Murray in the 1951 Broadway production of *The Rose Tattoo*.

Williams's use of symbols in this play includes the urn holding what Serefina believes are the ashes of her husband's body. Since he was burned after being shot and crashing his truck, the priest considers these ashes as a cremation, which was at that time against church rules. However, holding onto what she believes are his ashes helps Serefina keep the illusion of his faithfulness and presence in her life. When the truth is known to Serefina, she flings the urn, which cracks and lets the ashes blow away on the wind. It occurs to her that these ashes as well as the plastic statue of the Virgin Mary, may symbolize a faith that was not real, that was misplaced. Or perhaps Rosario's love—and that of the Virgin Mary—were far greater than her simple comprehension? One of Williams's favorite symbols is the lit candle. Serefina constantly lights candles to the Madonna. Yet she refuses to see the light of truth about her husband.

Another interesting symbol is the gold ring that Jack wears in his pierced ear, which for a sailor symbolizes his crossing the equator. At the end of their time together, when Jack must ship out, Rosa begs: "I want you to give me that little gold ring on your ear to put on my finger—I want to give you my heart to keep forever and ever!"[9] Now the gold ring, which as always meant fidelity, will symbolize this couples' crossing "the equator" of a more adult relationship.

An annoying goat boldly roams the yards and homes of Serefina's neighborhood. Critics called the goat "an emblem of the play's lyric spirit—the Dionysian element in human life, its mystery, its beauty, its significance."[10] As with all of Williams's symbols, the goat also adds to the realistic element, as Sicilian families often kept a goat for milk and cheese.

The title symbol of the play, the rose tattoo, can have several interpretations. It is referred to so often in this play that it almost becomes comic. Serefina's husband had a rose tattooed on his chest, which so fascinated her that for a moment she saw it burn on her own breast. The rose was to Serefina the symbol of their desire. By later in the play, when her prospective lover Alvaro wants to attract her, he gets a rose tattooed on his own chest. Serafina accuses this tactic as a ruse, a way to deceive her. Of course, it was her first husband who was the deceiver, for he committed adultery. It is Alvaro that sincerely wants to be true to her. So what does the rose symbolize? In this context, the rose can represent sexual beauty—purity—as well as the conception of a new life.

The Night of the Iguana Pits People on the Edge

This complex drama is considered Williams's last great Broadway triumph. *The Night of the Iguana* creates a strange world all its own for its characters to inhabit. In 1940, Maxine is managing the Costa Verde Hotel with her Mexican boy assistants. Into the hilltop resort come groups from other worlds: Nazis from Germany, Baptist teachers and students from Texas led by the desperately troubled Reverend Shannon, and artists like Hannah and her ninety-seven-year-old grandfather, Nonno, from Nantucket. Williams asks us to quickly accept this crowd of misfits. The survivors are separated from those who are at the end of their tether, but all have fascinating stories and actions to reveal.

When we get to know Shannon and Hannah, we realize they should have had more options. Like Williams, their lives have become ones of restless roaming, until they run out of money and survival tactics. Williams called Shannon, Hannah, and Nonno world-conquered protagonists. Shannon fights the "spooks" of depression and alcoholism, while Hannah quietly sips opium tea. Shannon quit being a true minister because of "fornication and heresy, in the same week."[11] His doubt and distrust of God and his weakness for girls have driven him to a breakdown. Hannah asks to lead him beside still waters. She has little else to give him. Yet Shannon calls her a real lady, and a great one.

As the play nears a climax, Shannon is tied to the crossbar of a hammock, for he has threatened suicide. Hannah accuses him of putting on a "Passion Play" performance. He is atoning for his sins here instead of on a cross with nails. However, her kindness, strength, and understanding give Shannon hope. She echoes the author's personal moral code when she tells Shannon nothing human disgusts me, unless it's unkind, violent.

Nonno finally completes his last great poem, a plea for courage in the face of the natural corruption and decay of mankind. Shannon agrees to Hannah's request: He cuts loose the iguana tied up to be eaten by the boys, "so that one of God's creatures could scramble home safe and free . . . a little act of grace."[12] At the play's end, Shannon compromises himself for a safe life with Maxine. Nonno has passed away. Hannah looks to God for rest and peace at last.

Symbols Right Up Top

Like *The Rose Tattoo*, Williams has put his primary symbol into the title. *The Night of the Iguana* refers both to the dark night of the spirit and to the captive lizard itself. In one sense, catching, fattening, and eating the iguana is a way of survival for the poor in Mexico. In another, the struggling iguana, says Shannon, is "at the end of its rope. Trying to go on past the end . . . like you! Like me! Like Grampa with his last poem!"[13] To free the iguana was a strike for freedom and hope for the future for Hannah and Shannon.

Because this play depended so much on symbols and metaphors, Williams said it was more of a dramatic poem than a play, using metaphorical ways of expression. Religious and Christian spiritual symbols are found everywhere. The Reverend Shannon nearly strangles himself trying to yank off his gold cross around his neck. And the bitter opium tea Hannah gives him as a compassionate offering is referred to as Christ's Communion cup. Williams noted in his *Selected Essays* that "some critics resent my symbols, but where would I be without them? . . . unless the events of a life are translated into significant meanings, then life holds no more revelation than death."[14]

Critic Howard Taubman saw Williams "writing at the top of his form" in *Iguana*. "He is still grappling with the human mysteries that have always haunted him."[15] Taubman concludes that the play is eloquent in "declaring its respect for those who have to fight for their bit of decency."[16]

All of Williams's major plays studied so far have explored a wider range and depth of human character than the plays written by most of his contemporaries. Williams said in an essay: "[T]he theater has made in our time its greatest artistic advance through the unlocking and lighting up and ventilation of the closets, attics, and basements of human behavior and experience."[17] Looking back, Williams was perhaps more important than any other author in creating this "lighting up" on stage.

NOTABLE WORKS TAKE ON POETIC THEMES: *CAMINO REAL*, *SUDDENLY LAST SUMMER*, AND *SWEET BIRD OF YOUTH*

I can't expose a human weakness on the stage unless I know it through having it myself.

—Tennessee Williams in the Foreword to *Sweet Bird of Youth*[1]

One of the one-acts Williams wrote in 1948 was expanded into a long play that is unlike any other. He called it *Camino Real*. When it opened on Broadway in March 1953, a lot of Williams's political criticism was cut out. He had written of the unchecked power of capitalism and the activities of a government committee that investigated people's political and personal lives. The rest of the play, expressionistic and dreamlike in structure, was filled with literary figures like Casanova, Marguerite Gautier, or "Camille," Lord Byron, Kilroy, and Don Quixote. It also portrayed average people struggling through a hard life, such as gypsies, street cleaners, loan sharks, and vendors. In order to give the sense of freedom and flow, Williams said he had to pay "more conscious attention to form and construction than I have in any work before. Freedom is not achieved simply by working freely."[2]

After the Broadway audiences failed to flow along with Williams and this play as presented, he rewrote it his way. Several characters and scenes and presumably the more politically critical material were restored for its 1953 publication and remain today.

Suddenly Last Summer Opens Off Broadway with *Something Unspoken*

Williams endured many personal problems during the late 1950s, including the psychiatric breakdown of his mother and

Hurd Hatfield, center, plays the part of Lord Byron in one of the dream sequences in *Camino Real*.

the death of his father. When Frank Merlo found him impossible to live with, Williams finally began psychiatric treatment himself. Throughout all of the hardships, he somehow found the drive to keep writing. *Suddenly Last Summer* and *Sweet Bird of Youth* were written between *Rose Tattoo* and *Night of the Iguana*. They showed that during the worst of times, Tennessee Williams could still be the best of writers.

Suddenly Last Summer, a powerful drama that consisted of seventy-five pages, seemed to need a companion piece to make audiences feel they had gotten a full evening at the theater. Although a show running an hour and a half with an intermission is acceptable today, Williams published *Suddenly Last Summer* with a short piece called *Something Unspoken*. Only the first show has maintained critical and audience interest. It remains one of the most bizarre and highly discussed work by any twentieth century playwright.

How the Setting Sets Us Up

The setting for *Suddenly Last Summer* is described at the start of the play in Williams's usual detail. We are told we are in a New Orleans Garden District Victorian mansion—yet the class and charm of such a locale is unseen. The mansion's garden/conservatory is tropical, almost prehistoric, "inhabited by beasts, serpents, and birds, all of a savage nature."[3] This is the home of Violet Venable, a name that sounds almost like "venerable," a fierce, domineering, and slightly disabled widow. We learn this strange garden filled with carnivorous plants was maintained by Violet's late son Sebastian, whom Violet describes to the visiting Dr. Cukrowitz as a poet, whose life was his occupation. Sets are usually important to Williams, along with lighting, sound effects, and music. In *Suddenly*, they also indicate the level of unreality and fear that is to come.

Characters Keep Us Guessing

Besides Violet Venable and Dr. Cukrowitz, we soon meet the beautiful Catharine Holly (Violet's niece) and her mother and brother, who are greedy, almost cartoonish clod-like Southerners. How the Holly family became entwined in Violet and Sebastian's unnatural life together requires the audience to swallow a fair amount of discomfort and disbelief. Yet audience members arrive knowing this is Tennessee Williams's fantasy, and somewhere in Violet, Catharine, and the ghostly presence of Sebastian, people sense they are seeing a vision of Edwina, Rose, and Tom.

Are Violet and Catharine reliable narrators? Should their varying versions of Sebastian's character, life, and murder be believed? The facts as related by Violet are fairly unbelievable—she claims that for twenty-five years she and Sebastian traveled continually, and that Sebastian lived a chaste life, although pursued by handsome young people. She claimed "we would carve out each day of our lives like a piece of sculpture. Yes we left behind us a trail of days like a gallery of sculpture!"[4] The doctor seems to wonder why a handsome, wealthy man like Sebastian would want to spend his life physically and emotionally tied to his mother.

When Catharine starts to relate her journey with Sebastian the past summer to Cabeza de Lobo—her only summer with him since Violet had become too old and frail from a stroke to travel—we see that this narrator is also mentally upset. Can she be unreliable as well? As Catharine relates the core of the past action, which we will see only through her fantasy (since Violet refutes it and Sebastian is dead), she claims Sebastian was hardly chaste. He was an ordinary homosexual man, one who preferred young boys as he aged. Sebastian seemed to need a woman to attract them—a role which Violet played for him on their long summers at the world's beaches—but a role that he then asked Catharine to play. Most young gay prostitutes accept money for sex and hardly need a beautiful female to attract them. So, does the tale get darker? Had Sebastian actually raped boys who were not professionals? Did Catharine know? As for Violet, her unnatural attachment to Sebastian went the distance—she screams at Catharine: "He was mine! I knew how to help him, I could!"

All Catherine says is that Sebastian, who had heart disease and was taking pills to control it, had insisted they eat lunch at a beach café, where they were susceptible to a gang of naked beach boys who jeered him and made a racket on handmade metal drums and cymbals. Sebastian, whom she claimed never took any action about anything whatsoever—ordered the waiters to beat off the gang of noisemakers. Sebastian then decided to leave in spite of the heat, telling Catharine: "That gang of kids shouted vile things about me to the waiters!"[5]

Catharine and Sebastian could not climb the hill and outrun the beach boys—who converged on Sebastian. When Catharine returned with help, Sebastian had been stripped and murdered. The naked beach boys used their tin cymbals and instruments to slash him to death, even carving off parts of his body and committing cannibalism.

Violet demands the doctor perform a lobotomy on Catharine to remove the gruesome tale of Sebastian's life and death. The doctor reflects to himself and the audience: "I think we ought at least to consider the possibility that the girl's story could be true . . ."[6]

When we use people solely for sex, Williams seems to ask, are we devouring them—or being spiritually devoured? Although there is absolutely no information that Williams ever used underage boys for sex, the boys in Catharine's story were not only underage but starving and unsupported. If Sebastian had used them, it was their turn to use him as prey. Or could Sebastian be seen as a symbol of sacrifice—as in ancient times when animals were slain and eaten raw?

Suddenly was so fascinating in all its possibilities as well as its lyrical dialogue, that its off-Broadway production did well, and brought the Obie Award to Anne Meacham as Catharine. Williams and his fellow author Gore Vidal then wrote a screenplay version, which had to be greatly expanded. But the authors failed to get their way with the censors of the time. In

Some of Hollywood's biggest names starred in the 1959 film version of *Suddenly Last Summer*; shown here are, from left to right, Katharine Hepburn, Mongomery Clift, and Eizabeth Taylor.

his *New York Times* review, Bosley Crowther said of the film that without clear information of Sebastian's homosexuality, how or why the beach boys killed him, and visual details of his death, the core of the play's meaning was lost. The film's stars—Elizabeth Taylor, Katharine Hepburn, and Montgomery Clift—were all at times the best film actors in America. Not this time, said Mr. Crowther. He criticized Taylor's Catharine in the finale as "sheer histrionic showing off," Hepburn for using "bony and bumptious posturing," and Clift for looking "racked with pain and indifference."[7]

Audiences disagreed. Both Taylor and Hepburn got Academy Award nominations for Best Actress in a Leading Role—very rare to happen in the same film. The play finally received a Broadway debut in 1995, performing with *Something Unspoken*, at the Circle in the Square Theatre.

Sweet Bird of Youth Flies High

The tale of Alexandra Del Lago, an aging, failed movie star, and Chance Wayne, a poor small-town actor who will do anything to make it, plus retrieve Heavenly, the girl he loved as a teen, was a long time in coming to Broadway. From 1955 Williams workshopped the script, including a Miami production starring Tallulah Bankhead. The play finally opened in New York in March 1959 starring Geraldine Page, Paul Newman, Diana Hyland, and Sidney Blackmer. Future stars Rip Torn and Bruce Dern played smaller roles. Williams was glad to have his favorite director/designer team Elia Kazan and Jo Mielziner to create *Sweet Bird*'s virgin flight.

The Findley family of *Sweet Bird* bears a certain resemblance to the Pollitt family of *Cat on a Hot Tin Roof*. "Boss" Findley is as rude and domineering as Big Daddy Pollitt. The Findley offspring, Tom Jr. and Heavenly, are totally dominated by their politically powerful father, who never shows any real love for them. This is where the resemblance between the two plays ends, for in spite of his overbearing ways and desire to run his plantation until the day he dies, Big Daddy does care for his children, and wants the best for his daughter-in-law Maggie. Although Big Daddy is often impatient and bossy with his wife, he seems true to her. Boss Findley is unlikeable to the core. His wife does not even appear in the play—but her replacement, Findley's mistress, Lucy, is a well-rounded character who gives sage advice to Chance and Heavenly.

The play is set in what must be considered "Findley's town" of St. Cloud, on the Gulf Coast. For reasons not quite clear, Williams informs us that the time of this play is "modern, an Easter Sunday, from morning until late night."[8]

Some reflections from previous great plays occur in the characters of Alexandra and Chance. Alexandra and Chance are originals, yet some might see a bit of Blanche du Bois in Alexandra. Both are losing the bloom of youth and feel they may be at the end of their road. But Alexandra was a dedicated actress and manages to make what a Hollywood columnist called "the greatest comeback in the history of the industry."[9] Alexandra has been using Chance as her paid driver and male companion. Chance has been using Alexandra in return as a ticket to money and glamour in show business. When Chance tries to bully Alexandra into pushing a movie career for him and Heavenly, she says to him: "I climbed back alone up the beanstalk to the ogre's country where I live, now, alone. Chance, you've gone past something you couldn't afford to go past; your time, your youth."[10]

Some critics note that a theme in this play is that of spiritual decline due to the powerful desire for fame and its demands. Although Alexandra seems strong enough to live with her fame, this desire is eating up Chance Wayne. Did Williams himself wonder if this decline was happening to him?

When her taxi arrives to get her to the nearest airport, Alexandra has one last moment of sympathy for Chance—but he will not go with her to escape his fate. As Alexandra leaves, Chance is surrounded by Boss Findley's son and his thugs, who will surely physically destroy him. Chance ends by addressing the audience: "I don't ask for your pity, just your understanding, not even that—no. Just for your recognition of me in you, and the enemy, time, in us all."[11]

Chance Wayne has shown both a pathetic side and a cruel one—he tries blackmail and bullying to get his way with Alexandra. Apparently he has given venereal disease to Heavenly during their one time as lovers (although she was spirited away so no one knew except her family). Chance is almost an anti-hero, trying to claw his way up from poverty, but damaging those he encounters on the way.

This play ran for a solid 375 performances. When the 1959 Tony Award nominations came out, *Sweet Bird of Youth* received four, including Geraldine Page for Best Actress. Unexpectedly, Paul Newman was not nominated for playing the extremely difficult role of Chance Wayne. He did win the part in the movie version, which helped his rise to stardom. The play was revived in 1975, and again the stars were nominated for Tonys in a revival. Only the actress playing Alexandra—Irene Worth—won the prize.

As for Tennessee Williams, the success of this difficult play in 1959, plus some of his new film versions, had him say to his closest colleague Elia Kazan: "I'm SCARED. . . Out of my fright, as much as out of my love of creation, now, I am still working compulsively. . . The question is if I go on this way, how long can I do so?"[12]

Williams in His "Stoned Age"

Tennessee Williams had been working on a play called *The Milk Train Doesn't Stop Here Anymore* in 1962. After the death from cancer of his longtime companion Frank Merlo in September 1963, *Milk Train* opened off Broadway. Williams had been too absorbed with the illness of his fifteen-year companion to worry about what he considered a workshop production.

After Frank's family gave him a requiem mass, Williams moved the body to a funeral home on Madison Avenue. There a special guest list of all their friends and colleagues heard the eulogy that Williams personally wrote for Frank. Although Williams was too sad to read it, a relative named Reverend Sidney Lanier did so. Williams called Merlo's honorable, inalterable character "A source of unfailing reassurance as a beacon of light in a harbor."[13]

pathos

An element in creative art or experience that evokes sympathy, pity, and/or compassion. The adjective is pathetic.

Milk Train may have been the worst received of any Williams Broadway premiere. The show opened on January 1, 1964—and closed on the third. The lead performances of Tallulah Bankhead and Tab Hunter had a lot to do with its failure. However, as he got past the embarrassment of *Milk Train*'s quick demise, Williams may have realized that the character of Flora Goforth might be the closest to his own interior self. Through her character, Williams expresses his loss and grief over Merlo's death and his guilt over their being estranged before Merlo was stricken with cancer.

In his *Memoirs*, Williams recalled: "What I didn't know was that I was as much in love with Frankie all that difficult time of the early Sixties as I had even been before."[14] He later reflected: "[W]hen he ceased to be alive, I couldn't create a life for myself. So I went into a seven-year depression."[15] Williams referred to this period as "my stoned age."[16] His addiction to a combination of prescription drugs began to destroy him, a situation obvious to everyone close to him.

In 1969, Tennessee's brother, Dakin, stepped in to help save his brother. Dakin encouraged him to be confirmed into the Roman Catholic Church, a religion Dakin had joined when in the service. After Tennessee received the sacraments, Dakin forced his brother into Barnes Hospital in St. Louis for detoxification and therapy. The hospital staff felt he would be best treated in the psychiatric ward. This hospital stay was terrifying for Williams. He knew that both his sister and his mother had been committed for mental illness, and he feared his own mental breakdown. Dakin Williams's intervention may have saved his brother's life. Yet Tennessee said he was traumatized over it. He never accepted the good reasons why Dakin did this, and he broke relations with him. In fact, the treatment granted Williams sufficient physical and mental strength to continue writing for another two decades.

The Seventies: Williams's Age of Experimentation

Later scripts came in abundance. Critic Philip C. Kolin notes that: "Williams' later plays outnumber those of the 1940s and the 1950s. These later works may be regarded as postmodern canvasses on which Williams was painting the agony of his canon."[17] Kolin also noted these plays' emphasis on transformation and transcendence.

Two of Williams's early works of the seventies were *Small Craft Warnings* (opened off Broadway April 2, 1972, then at the New Theatre in June 1972) and *Red Devil Battery Sign* (opened in Boston June 18, 1976). *Small Craft Warnings*, set in a seedy beachfront bar north of San Diego, is an expanded version of a one-act play called *Confessional*. Some of its characters are grounded, such as Monk the bar owner and Leona and Doc, who are local residents. Others are just drifting through. Doc tells Monk: "You are running a place of refuge for vulnerable human vessels."[18] Characters take turns in a "confessional area" under a special spotlight where they tell

In a 1972 off-Broadway production, Williams himself played the role of Doc in *Small Craft Warnings* opposite Gene Fanning as Monk the bartender.

the audience directly how they feel about their lives. Three of the male characters are gay, and two take advantage sexually of unstable female characters. The language can be vulgar, the action violent. Tennessee Williams himself played the role of the drunken, unlicensed Doc in the first week's performances to excite business. The dark radical nature of the play failed to impress critics, but it intrigued audiences enough to give it a solid two-hundred-performance run.

Red Devil Battery Sign reflects some of the social and political concerns that Williams expressed as far back as the 1950s. The theme is entrapment of people by their own needs and by the materialist industrial culture that runs America. Williams was actually forward-looking in the 1970s to envision how the mechanized world might soon paralyze human self-expression and interrelationships. Companies had begun to depend on computers. To a man who had always been suspicious of Big Business, this development was worrisome. Director Ed Sherin, who worked on the 1976 Boston production, said: "To me the play was the most important work of the decade, with a clear warning to our society about the destructive force of unbridled corporate power."[19]

A theme also runs through *Red Devil* regarding America's deep military involvement in Vietnam, a situation Williams protested. Set in contemporary Dallas, the characters are given characteristic names like King. They are difficult to analyze and not always appealing. Yet the story is a fine attempt to define the role of secrets, money, and power in life. As Woman Downtown, the leading female character, says: "It talks, money talks, not heads, not hearts, not tongues of prophets or angels, but money does, oh money hollers, love."[20]

Sometimes innovative plays come far ahead of their time. *Red Devil Battery Sign* was produced in Boston, June 1974, and in London, June 1977, a period when theater-goers and critics did not care for its message. It has never had a Broadway production.

Next, Williams decided to write a deeply revealing autobiography. Working with editors from Doubleday and Company, he produced *Memoirs* in 1975. In this rambling, chaotic book, Williams gave shocking information about his emotional problems, addictions, and sexual habits. Critics wished it had revealed more about his writing life and career. It did capture much of Williams's dark humor and honesty.

The one constant thing in Williams's life was movement. He moved between his regular haunts of Key West, New Orleans, and New York, running to Europe to see productions of his plays. He regularly visited his sister, Rose, in her care facility in Ossining, New York. Sometimes he had Rose driven to New York City for a treat. In 1975, he told his longtime friends director Elia Kazan and actress Maureen Stapleton that his one obligation was to endure.

Williams Returns "Home" to New Orleans and St. Louis

Two of Williams's home cities were the sites for his late plays. *Vieux Carré* was set during Williams's early years in New Orleans. It ran well in London in 1978, but it was never a Broadway success. *A Lovely Sunday for Creve Coeur*, which opened off Broadway in 1979, was set in his old neighborhood in St. Louis. By setting *Creve Coeur* in the 1930s, Williams could use his personal memories of the city's social attitudes and locales.

A *Lovely Sunday for Creve Coeur* can be seen as a string quartet, made up of four women's voices. Dorothea, a lonely, thirtyish, high school civics teacher, speaks with the violin's melody. Bodey, nearly forty, a hardworking factory clerk, underscores a hardy bass. Art teacher Helena, an affected, snobbish spinster, insinuates the viola's sound. And Sophie Gluck, an emotionally disturbed, grieving girl living in Dorothea and Bodey's building, moans and cries like the cello. These four women are intertwined in their needs and goals. Some goals seem to be selfish, some driven by fear. By the drama's end, those who deserve lasting love and caring will receive them.

As this work was previewing in New York, Tennessee Williams joined a group interview for New York Theatre Review. Director Craig Anderson liked *A Lovely Sunday for Creve Coeur* because "the women are the most beautiful characterizations. This play is simply lovely in the way that the three women vie for each other's favor."[21] Williams recognized that these women were ordinary, down-to-earth Midwesterners. He did not write long speeches with poetic or lyrical imagery. He said, "If I had put lyricism into the mouths of any of those characters, it would have been out of character, it wouldn't have rung true."[22] This shows Williams never lost his clear regard for each character as a singular individual.

Williams applied his usual "red pen" on the revision process on *Creve Coeur*. Director Anderson called him a "rewrite specialist," and claimed he gave more than is needed to cut away, "down to the bare bone of what needs to stay."[23] While Williams stated that "loneliness is the main theme," he also saw valor as a recurring characteristic in the play. He talked about Dorothea, who finally realizes her lover, Ralph, has used her sexually and then dumped her. Williams has Dorothea tell Sophie Gluck, "Now, Sophie, we just have to go on. That's all life seems to offer or demand, just go on."[24]

Williams himself went on, even when the core of his life, his plays, seemed to be rejected by the critics. In 1981, he gave an interview to his friend, journalist Dotson Rader. He was at work on what would be his final full play, *A House Not Meant to Stand*. He told Rader: "When I write, I don't aim to shock people . . . I don't think that anything that occurs in life should be omitted from art, though the artist should present it in a fashion that is artistic and not ugly. I set out to tell the truth. And sometimes the truth is shocking."[25]

When Rader asked Williams how he regarded death, he said, "I have a very strong will. There were occasions in the last years when I might have gone out. But my will forces me to go on because I've got unfinished work."[26]

Tennessee Williams died late on the night of February 24, 1983. Police found him in his New York hotel suite, with a medicine bottle cap lodged inside his throat. Conflicting reports were published on what happened. However, Williams's death was ruled to have been a choking accident.

How Great Playwrights Influence Each Other: What Williams Took From Ibsen, Strindberg, Chekhov, and O'Neill

During much of his life, Tennessee Williams kept what he called "Notebooks." Unlike the multitude of letters he sent over forty years to friends and colleagues [many of whom carefully saved them and had them printed after Williams's death], these Notebooks preserved his thoughts, feelings, ideas, and bits of conversations. In 1941 he recorded an exchange with Professor Oliver Evans, a gay man who had become a good friend through their vacations in Provincetown. Evans struggled with guilt and self-loathing over his sexual orientation. Williams had the opposite feeling: "To feel some humiliation . . . is inevitable. But feeling guilty is foolish. I am a deeper and warmer and kinder man for my deviation."[1] He believed that being part of his minority made him more conscious of need in others. "What power I have to express the human heart must be in large part due to this circumstance."[2]

No doubt Williams was sincere in his acceptance of his nature and even proud of how he was born. Yet as a new playwright, he had almost no gay predecessors in American

Williams was forced to break new ground as an openly gay playwright, but he found inspiration in writers who, like him, searched for the humanity in their characters.

theater. He admired poets Hart Crane, Walt Whitman, and D.H. Lawrence, who were gay or bisexual men, but never openly wrote about their orientation. So who could he look to for inspiration? He decided to seek those who, like him, were able to express the human heart.

During a summer visit with his grandparents in 1935, a Memphis theater group produced Williams's short play. He called it "a farcical but rather touching little comedy about two sailors on a date."[3] It was at that time, he said, "I fell in love with the writing of Anton Chekhov."[4] Williams claimed the Russian author "takes precedence as an influence—that is, if there has been any particular influence beside my own solitary bent."[5] Williams especially loved Chekhov's *The Seagull*, which he called the greatest of modern plays.

Anton Chekhov (1860–1904) was famed for both his short stories and full-length plays. Besides *The Seagull*, his most widely produced plays are *The Cherry Orchard*, *The Three Sisters*, and *Uncle Vanya*. Chekhov's characters are all small-town, middle-class folk. They are striving to move socially upward, lead a better life, and achieve goals. Yet they are trapped in their mundane rural existence. Based in nineteenth-century Russian society, these characters are limited by their social and economic class as much as by their lack of drive.

Theater scholar Oscar G. Brockett said of Chekhov's plays: "The subtext is often as important as text. . . . The plays intermingle the comic, serious, pathetic, and ironic so thoroughly that they do not fit into any dramatic type."[6] Williams felt the sense of frustration, loneliness, and family misunderstanding that pervades Chekhov's plays. He used it in shaping his own dramatic work.

Williams Finds Modernist Style in Europeans

August Strindberg of Sweden was considered a shocking radical by the turn of the twentieth century. He wrote plays exploring human relationships in a frank but realistic way. Few authors since Shakespeare had written about parental anger, sexual violence, and male-female struggles for power the way Strindberg did.

Henrik Ibsen of Norway took a different approach. He wrote about intense conflict between men and women, in an era when women were dominated by the males in their lives. He stripped away the exterior layer of people's social behavior. Forbidden subjects such as adultery, female suicide, divorce and family abandonment, and sexually transmitted diseases all figured in Ibsen's work.

Theater historian Peter Arnott said of Ibsen's play *A Doll's House* (1879–80), "So convincing was Ibsen's portrayal of a marriage that the audiences were shocked. This play seemed to reach into their own homes and threaten the foundations of society."[7] Ibsen's work was banned in his own country for many years. Williams found these Scandinavians liberating.

Eugene O'Neill: A Twentieth Century Predecessor to Williams

Williams was familiar with American playwright Eugene O'Neill's work. O'Neill was born in 1888 to a New York theater family. His father, James O'Neill, was a leading actor, and his brother also became one. Young Eugene was determined to write in a new style, different from the melo-dramas and romances in which his father starred. O'Neill took classic stories and portrayed them in radical, unusual ways. By studying new European authors, O'Neill used their nonrealistic methods to bring out the desires and fears of his

Eugene O'Neill, Williams's predecessor in twentieth-century theater, was innovative in his use of realism in drama. He often drew on his own difficult family relationships when developing his stories, much like Williams did with *The Glass Menagerie*.

characters. Like Strindberg, he explored dream sequences. He showed minds fragmenting and human guilt destroying people. Sometimes he used masks on his actors. To encourage actors to pronounce each word the way he wanted, O'Neill wrote in dialect for many of his characters. Often he used long interior monologues to express a character's feelings. He experimented constantly with shape, form, and style.

Some of O'Neill's important plays of the 1920s are not often produced today. Two of them, *Strange Interlude* (1928) and *Mourning Becomes Electra* (1931) are extremely long and dark. Other works use stories from New England, where the O'Neill family owned a summer cottage in New London, Connecticut. This simple house overlooking the sea was the only real home Eugene knew. He absorbed the ways of New England seafarers and farmers and colorful characters like those he met in the New London waterfront bars. These people found their way into his plays.

Desire Under the Elms (1924) is an American drama that reflects the classic Greek dramas of *Oedipus Rex* and *Phaedra*. O'Neill tells the tale of a tough old father, his beautiful younger new wife, and his adult sons. When the wife develops a passion for her stepson, tragedy is bound to happen. *A Moon for the Misbegotten, The Iceman Cometh*, and *Long Day's Journey Into Night* were all completed by 1940, when O'Neill fell ill. *Long Day's Journey* was not produced until after his death in 1953. It is a heartfelt study of O'Neill's frustrated, tyrannical father, sad, morphine-addicted mother, and alcoholic older brother. The younger brother with tuberculosis represents himself. This hurtful family is trapped together in their New London cottage. O'Neill won every playwriting major award, including one that was never given to any other American dramatist: the Nobel Prize for Literature.

No doubt the wide variety of techniques that O'Neill used influenced Williams. In a 1981 interview, Williams said: "I liked O'Neill's writing. He had . . . a great sense of drama, yes. But most of all, it was his spirit, his passion, that moved me."[8] O'Neill's major work was available in the 1920s through the 1940s, all Williams's formative years as a playwright.

O'Neill proved that America could produce a great, enduring, original playwright. He must have given Williams hope to go on exploring.

What Playwrights Took from Tennessee Williams

William Inge

Two years after Tennessee Williams was born in Columbus, Mississippi, William Inge was born in 1913 and raised in Independence, Kansas. In 1915, Arthur Miller was born in New York City and raised in Brooklyn. These three writers came from the same generation, but different regions, different backgrounds, and different religions. Yet they ended up producing Broadway shows and outstanding films that competed with and complemented each other for decades.

William Inge, like Williams and Miller, knew early in his life that he wanted to be a writer. Inge earned college degrees in Lawrence, Kansas, and Nashville, Tennessee, and taught both high school and college drama courses. Inge crossed paths with Tennessee Williams when Williams was still Tom in St. Louis. As a St. Louis newspaper drama critic, Inge reviewed Williams's plays and admired him. He went to Chicago to review *The Glass Menagerie*. He later said, "I was so moved by the play . . . I thought it was the finest play I had seen in many years. I went home to St. Louis and felt, 'Well, I've got to write a play.'"[9] Williams's method of using common family experiences inspired Inge, who said: "Now I know where to look for a play—inside myself."[10]

Inge's play *Come Back, Little Sheba*, opened on Broadway in 1950. Inge, like Williams, wrote about interpersonal relationships in humble homes. His intimate knowledge and understanding of people he credited to his family and friends in Independence. He said: "Big people come out of small towns."[11] *Come Back, Little Sheba*, a drama that brought lead actress Shirley Booth the Tony Award, centers on a middle-aged couple who married early because the woman was pregnant. "Doc" Delaney, a reformed alcoholic, had to give up medical school and support Lola, who lost the baby at birth. After years of dreary marriage, in which Lola heaped her affection on her little dog, Sheba, the couple rents a room to a beautiful college girl—and the inevitable sexual explosion occurs.

Williams admired Inge's work. He told Dotson Rader: "*Come Back, Little Sheba* was a brilliant play. That's why I introduced him to Audrey Wood."[12] Wood had become Inge's agent, and promoted his career with the same drive she gave to Williams.

In 1953, Inge's play *Picnic* ran on Broadway, winning the Pulitzer Prize, New York Drama Critics Circle Award, and many others. This warm family drama centers on women in a small Kansas town affected by the arrival of an attractive male stranger. Inge portrayed simple people who were deeply intertwined in one another's lives.

In 1955, Inge saw his play *Bus Stop* open on Broadway. A Midwestern comedy/drama about a handful of drifting souls stuck in a roadside café during a snowstorm, *Bus Stop* touched critics and audiences. It is perhaps his most revived play. *The Dark at the Top of the Stairs*, a 1957 autobiographical work in

William Inge (pictured) and Williams were friends who respected each other's work, although Inge never achieved Williams's level of fame.

which Inge again used family experiences, was a great critical success. Inge's 1959 play *A Loss of Roses* did not please the critics and had a short run.

Inge's tendency toward alcoholism and depression began to affect him. Sometimes critics, although admiring of Inge's works, called him "Williams Junior," which was unfortunate, given Inge's desire to become independently recognized. Williams tried to maintain the friendship with Inge that helped them both. When one enjoyed a success, the other fought jealousy; when one had a show get roasted, the other tried to be supportive. In the late 1960s in California, they even shared a personal psychiatrist.

Inge, like Williams, tried films. His original screenplay, *Splendor in the Grass*, starred young Natalie Wood, and in his first screen role, Warren Beatty. Inge himself played the small role of Reverend Whitman. Dealing with some of Tennessee Williams's favorite subjects—the battle in a young respectable girl to control her sexual passion, and the huge pressure placed on the favored son to carry on his father's dreams—Inge's characters were movingly portrayed. In 1960, Natalie Wood was nominated for Best Actress. Although she lost, Inge won the Academy Award for Best Original Screenplay.

Continuing as a playwright, Inge moved to California to teach. After writing two autobiographical novels, Inge succumbed to depression and alcoholism. He committed suicide in 1973.

Arthur Miller

Arthur Miller had a strong, varied career that lasted throughout the twentieth century until his death in February 2005 at age ninety. After graduating from the University of Michigan with some playwriting awards in hand, Miller returned to his native New York City. He married in 1940 and worked on building ships in the Brooklyn Navy Yard during World War II. The WPA's Federal Theatre Project gave him work as a radio scriptwriter. Although his first play done in New York was not successful, it won the Theatre Guild National Prize.

During 1945, Miller published his first novel, *Focus*. At this time, he saw *A Glass Menagerie* on Broadway. Miller said in a 1984 interview soon after Williams's death that this play "lifted lyricism to its highest level in our theatre's history . . . what was new in Tennessee Williams was his rhapsodic insistence that form serve his utterance rather than dominating and cramping it."[13] He showed poor ordinary people like the Wingfield family could be moving.

Miller wrote *All My Sons* in 1947, his first hit on Broadway. Also heavily influenced by Ibsen's plays, Miller showed his characters' prehistory in the way Ibsen did. Since he was writing about the consequences of men's actions, he needed to show what they had done before they appeared in the play's present. The play also explored the theme of the impact of a lost son.

In 1949, Miller's next important play, *Death of a Salesman*, opened. The salesman is Willy Loman, an older man who traveled New England to promote a company's products to dealers. Using a technique Miller might have seen in O'Neill's early plays, he has Willy Loman hear and speak to people from his past. Willy and the audience see these people, but no one else on stage does. This ranting leads his wife and sons to fear he is losing his mind. The decline and fall of Willy Loman, who determines all self-worth by being financially successful and being well-liked, becomes an American tragedy. This play brought Miller the Drama Critics Circle award and the

Pulitzer Prize. Tennessee Williams attended this production, and noted that the final scene was one of the best he had seen on stage.

The Crucible opened on Broadway in 1952. Miller had studied historic accounts of the Salem, Massachusetts, witch trials. He created a dramatic account of a Salem witch hunt to parallel an investigation of supposed Communists being done in 1950 by the House Un-American Activities Committee in Washington. Critic Raymond Williams says about *The Crucible*: "Miller brilliantly expresses a particular crisis—the modern witch hunt—in his own society. . . . It is not often that issues and statements so clearly emerge in a naturally dramatic form."[14] *The Crucible* won the Tony and the Donaldson Prize for 1953, and is often revived today.

In 1947, Miller wrote a one-act play based on a supposedly true story of an Italian longshoreman who informed on an illegal alien relative. In 1955, *A View from the Bridge*, paired with another one-act called *A Memory of Two Mondays*, opened on Broadway. Although it ran for 158 performances, critics did not care for what they called a cold and unengaging play. Miller expanded *A View from the Bridge* into a conventional two-act, and took it to London, where it was a hit with a new ending in which the informer protagonist Eddie is forgiven by his wife. Miller then took the play to Paris, where he wrote a third ending, in which Eddie commits suicide. Like Tennessee Williams, Miller was fascinated with ethnic culture (see *A Rose Tattoo*) and with continually revising his work.

Miller wrote throughout his later life. *After the Fall*, about his marriage to movie star Marilyn Monroe, and *Incident at Vichy* (1964), reflecting his views of anti-Jewish behavior, were both produced in New York. He wrote *The Price* in 1968, which was a Broadway success. *The Creation of the World and*

Williams enjoys the company of famed director Elia Kazan (*center*) and Arthur Miller (*right*). Kazan directed the works of both playwrights.

Other Business (1972), and *The American Clock* (1980) also had New York runs. Although his original screenplay *The Misfits* was not a success, his script *Playing for Time*, produced as a television film in 1980, was acclaimed. It portrayed the determination of concentration-camp women to stay alive by playing in an orchestra for their vicious captors.

In 1994, Miller saw his psychological drama *Broken Glass* premiere. This play unravels the many reasons why a Jewish New Yorker in 1938 may find her legs paralyzed. Miller explores the effects on his protagonist Sylvia of Nazi anti-Semitism, a husband who has turned his back on his Jewish identity, and a desperate need for attention. In 2000, Miller's final major work, *The Ride Down Mount Morgan*, appeared on Broadway. A tale of a rich and self-centered man who secretly juggles two wives and families, *The Ride* was both tragic and darkly comic at the same time.

Edward Albee

Born in 1928, Edward Albee was living in New York City during the 1950s when Williams, Inge, and Miller were hit playwrights. Albee was the adopted only child of the wealthy Albee family of Larchmont, New York, owners of a chain of theaters. Young Edward had a troubled youth. He disliked his parents, performed badly at several private high schools, and dropped out of college after his freshman year. Unlike Williams, who spent his twenties trying to write while nearly starving, Albee had a monthly inheritance on which to survive. He studied Williams's work and that of avant garde playwrights. Then he found his own unique style and voice.

Albee could be called a selective realist in the way that O'Neill, Miller, and Williams are. Selective realism is seen when a playwright sets his play in a real place, such as a house,

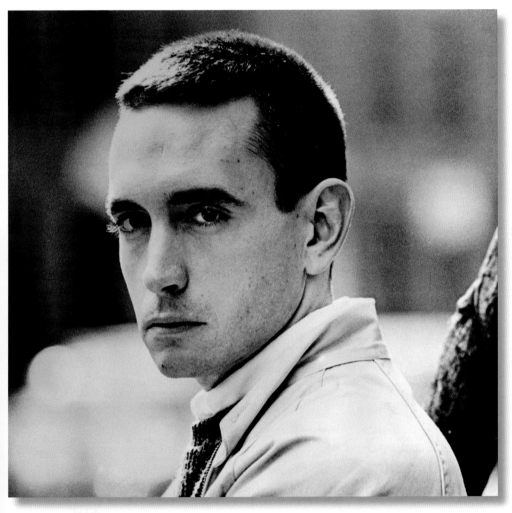

Playwright Edward Albee was a colleague and friend of Williams, of whom he said, "His personality was far more complex than the public image personality that we have of Tennessee."

a garden, a park, the beach, etc. He uses real people as characters. He then uses certain details of dialogue, sets, lights, or action in a way that is not realistic. Having the character Tom move back and forth between Narrator and family character in *The Glass Menagerie*, or having someone speak to or hear from others that are not present like Willie Loman does in *Death of a Salesman*, creates selective realism. Albee took this style to another level. He added the absurdist element. This meant that certain realistic characters suddenly say or do abnormal, nonsensical things. Absurdist writers use as a theme the lack of logic or sense in much of human relationships.

Albee's first works were short plays. In some ways they were funny, touching, even frightening. *The Zoo Story* opened off Broadway in January 1960. In April 1960, *The Sandbox* opened off Broadway and *The Death of Bessie Smith* opened in Berlin. These plays were filled with sharp dialogue and black humor. Critic and biographer Mel Gussow called *The Zoo Story* "a report from the front line of urban life and death."[15]

Nothing from these short plays quite prepared the theater world for Albee's first major work, *Who's Afraid of Virginia Woolf?* This lengthy three-act play opened on Broadway in the fall of 1962. It is set on a college campus (although Albee only spent a year and a half at Trinity College in Hartford, Connecticut) and explores an intense, bizarre marriage (although Albee was homosexual).

A long-married academic couple employs cruel games during an evening of heavy drinking with a new, young professor and his wife. We see that the older couple (George and Martha) cannot go on together without fights, humiliations, victories, and illusions. Albee said about this couple: "George and Martha enjoyed their verbal duels with each other, and while they were deadly serious, they were always . . . in admiration of each other's skills."[16]

The most baffling illusion George and Martha create is Sonny-Jim, their secret child, who represents the one pure thing between them. Suddenly Martha drags him out in front of young couple Nick and Honey. Once this "son" was the glue in their barren marriage. Now that he is exposed, he must be expelled. Will Martha and George survive as a couple? After their long evening of lashing out, Martha says to Nick: "George . . . who keeps learning the games we play as quickly as I can change the rules; who can make me happy and I do not wish to be happy, and yes I do wish to be happy. George and Martha . . . sad, sad, sad."[17] The play closes with Martha clinging to George. We cannot be certain of their future.

Critic David A. Crespy makes a good comparison between parts of *Who's Afraid of Virginia Wolf?* with *Streetcar Named Desire*. In both plays, we see the symbol-loaded event of a birthday party. In these plays, Blanche's southern belle dreams and Martha's imaginary son's existence are crushed by the supposed party. Blanche's desired guest Mitch turns her down, and her gift is a one-way bus ticket back to Mississippi. Martha's "party" is spoiled when George announces the "son" has been killed. Speech fails Blanche and Martha, Crespy reminds us, when the last of their illusions are crushed: "Language has been the mask, the means of keeping up the illusions, and in the end it must be destroyed."[18]

Albee has written many other plays on a variety of issues during his forty-year career. His themes have covered the breakdown in human communication (*Seascape*), man's attempt to understand God (*Tiny Alice*), and the many views of a woman's life (*Three Tall Women*). In a recent play, *Sylvia, or The Goat*, Albee creates a solid prosperous unit of the

Husband, Wife, Son, and Best Friend. He then pushes them over the edge, when the Husband develops a deep passion outside his marriage. This common infidelity becomes absurd and frightening when we find out his passion is for a docile goat called Sylvia.

At this publishing, Edward Albee is eighty-eight years old and still active.

Eugene O'Neill, William Inge, Arthur Miller, Edward Albee, and Tennessee Williams created a huge and varied body of theatrical work that has represented twentieth-century America, with Albee's work moving into the twenty-first. Although O'Neill was the leader, Williams by both importance and volume was probably the most influential in inspiring the other three. These authors' great plays are revived in theaters in America and around the world through the twenty-first century.

WILLIAMS'S WORK LIVES ON: THE LEGACY OF TENNESSEE WILLIAMS THROUGH REVIVAL AND FILM

I am frightened as ever of the critics. I am personally ready to have a final showdown with them before . . . emigrating to Australia because of an unremitting barrage of excrement from those or those who employ them.

—Tennessee Williams in a 1977 letter to director Arthur Allen Seidelman[1]

When he was alive Tennessee Williams often got caught in an ongoing war with drama critics. Of course, after he had passed away, the critics still did their work upon him—but he no longer cared.

The major sources that help us appreciate the body of Tennessee Williams's work, besides the published texts, are stage revivals and films. At the latest count, seventeen of Williams's works have been made into films. One, *Baby Doll*, combined two early short plays, and after being written as a film script, morphed into a full-length stage play. Williams himself worked on screenplays for *The Glass Menagerie*, *A Streetcar Named Desire*, *The Rose Tattoo*, *Baby Doll*, *The Fugitive Kind*, *Suddenly Last Summer*, and *Boom!* Other film versions had no input from the playwright. Although this total does not make Williams the king of stage-to-film—that honor belongs to American playwright Neil Simon, who had an amazing total of twenty-eight plays made into movies—it is still one of the greatest bodies of work made available to audiences today. This total does not include the films that were made directly for television production, many of which were critically acclaimed.

Williams's style of writing worked well for cinema directors. However, two stumbling blocks kept some of these films from being fully realized versions of Williams's work. First, films made in the 1950s and 1960s had to pass through a Hollywood censor's office. Adult dialogue, suggestive material, and visually explicit scenes had to be edited or cut out. Movie ratings did not exist as we know them today, so all films were available to the whole family. The Legion of Decency, run by the Roman Catholic Church, tried to weed out the ones that were inappropriate for the young. Second, some of Williams's poetic imagery and surrealistic interior monologues worked best on stage. There we accept people expressing themselves in an unreal manner. When blown up into a huge, realistic image on a movie screen, these kinds of self-expression often lose the playwright's meaning and even looked ludicrous.

A critique of these films will show how many succeeded in capturing the dramatic qualities Williams intended. Film critic and historian Leonard Maltin's *Classic Movie Guide* of 2015 is used as the primary source to document the films.

The Glass Menagerie (1950)

The first shot at filming a Williams play starred Gertrude Lawrence as Amanda, Kirk Douglas as Tom, and Jane Wyman as Laura. Williams did not work on this script. He indicated he did not think this film captured the essence of the play and was furious at some of the censorship. Maltin agreed, calling it "More notable for its cast and intentions than its result."[2] The story was remade as a TV film in 1973, starring Katharine Hepburn as Amanda, Sam Waterston as Tom, and Joanna

Williams arrives at the 1956 New York City premiere of *Baby Doll*. The film was produced by Williams and Elia Kazan and was nominated for four Academy Awards.

Miles as Laura. This film, directed by Anthony Harvey, was adapted by Williams. Maltin called it the "superior version."[3] In 1987, Paul Newman directed his wife, Joanne Woodward, as Amanda, John Malkovich as Tom, and Karen Allen as Laura in the latest film version.

A Streetcar Named Desire (1951)

Directed by Elia Kazan and scripted by Williams and Oscar Saul, this excellent recreation pushed Hollywood to new heights in adult material. In fact, critic R. Barton Palmer makes a case for *Streetcar* as the first true adult film made by mainstream Hollywood. "With its revelation and dramatization of sexual misconduct, its delineation of a horrifying descent into madness, its portrayal of women driven and even controlled by desire, the play offered themes that could not be accommodated" by the usual 1950 women's film with a happy ending.[4] Maltin called it "a stunning production."[5] It allowed adult filmgoers to use their intellects in understanding the leading characters, Stanley and Blanche, who are made up of both sympathetic and unsympathetic elements. It also studied the power and destructive nature of desire in a totally adult manner.

Marlon Brando as Stanley, Kim Hunter as Stella, Vivien Leigh as Blanche, and Karl Malden as Mitch made a perfect quartet. The movie received a record twelve Academy Award nominations, including Best Picture. "Oscars went to Leigh, Hunter and Malden for their flawless performances—as well as for the art direction-set direction."[6] This play was remade for television in 1984, starring Ann-Margret as Blanche, Treat Williams as Stanley, Beverly D'Angelo as Stella, and Randy Quaid as Mitch. Outstanding acting makes "this version stand proudly beside its classic predecessor."[7] The performance

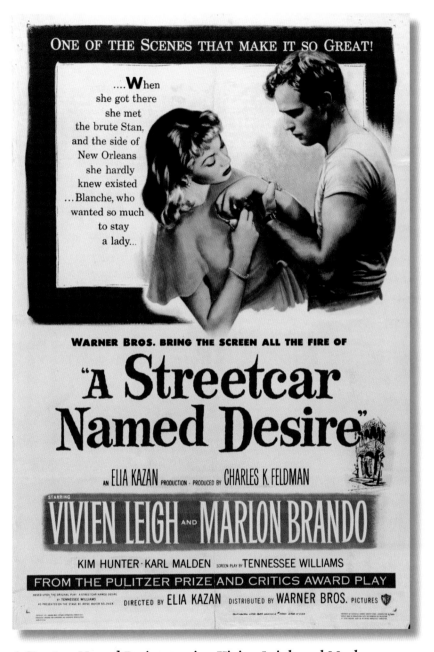

A Streetcar Named Desire starring Vivien Leigh and Marlon Brando was a critical success and established newcomer Brando as a major movie star.

never recognized by an award was Marlon Brando's—but Maltin noted he "left an indelible mark on audiences."[8]

The Rose Tattoo (1955)

Although Williams's friend, Italian actress Anna Magnani, was not a clear enough English speaker to land the Broadway role of Serefina (which went to the superb Maureen Stapleton), director Daniel Mann cast Magnani in his film version. His efforts with Magnani on dialogue paid off. Maltin said: "Magnani shines in [her] Oscar-winning role as an earthy, deluded widow."[9] Burt Lancaster played Alvaro, and Oscar nominee Marisa Pavan played the teenage daughter Rosa. The film was nominated for Best Picture. James Wong Howe won the Oscar for Best Cinematography.

Baby Doll (1956)

Williams wrote the screenplay with Elia Kazan as director. This film caused a furor for its sexual tension. Carroll Baker played the lead as Baby and won an Oscar nomination. Karl Malden played her husband Archie. Mildred Dunnock was also Oscar-nominated for her role as the aging servant based on Aunt Rose. Eli Wallach and Rip Torn made their film debuts. Unusual for its time was the stark, black-and-white, on-location filming in Mississippi. Maltin noted that the movie was condemned by the 1950s Legion of Decency: "Williams' story, although tame by today's standards, still sizzles."[10]

Cat on a Hot Tin Roof (1958)

Director Richard Brooks and James Poe wrote the adaptation. Elizabeth Taylor was cast as Maggie, Paul Newman as Brick, Burl Ives as Big Daddy, and Judith Anderson as Big Mama. Maltin said this "classic study of mendacity comes to the screen somewhat laundered but still packing a wallop; entire cast is sensational."[11] The film was nominated for Oscars as Best Picture, Best Actor, Best Actress, and Best Director—but none were winners.

Suddenly Last Summer (1959)

Williams's friend Gore Vidal was chosen to be the co-screenwriter. Joseph L. Mankiewicz directed. Katharine Hepburn as the wealthy, wicked Violet, and Elizabeth Taylor as her disturbed niece Catharine both got Best Actress nominations. This difficult, multilayered story with elements of sexual perversion, guilt, madness, and murder by cannibalism was difficult to film and had to be expanded and censored in ways that did not work. An excellent British film was made for television in 1992 starring Maggie Smith as Violet and Natasha Richardson as her niece. Maltin liked the British version and called the American one "fascinating if talky."[12]

The Fugitive Kind (1959)

In spite of its cast of experienced Williams players (Anna Magnani, Marlon Brando, Joanne Woodward, and Maureen Stapleton), and Williams as coauthor of the screenplay, the public did not support this film. Even the work of fine director Sidney Lumet did not make the film a success. Some critics, such as Bosley Crowther of the *New York Times*, felt it was an excellent version of his play, *Orpheus Descending*. However, Maltin said "the movie goes nowhere."[13]

The Roman Spring of Mrs. Stone (1961)

This film was made from Williams's novel of the same name, and it was reported to be his favorite. Although Lotte Lenya was nominated for Best Supporting Actress, the film's star, Vivien Leigh as Mrs. Stone, was passed over for nomination.

Summer and Smoke (1961)

Starring Geraldine Page, Laurence Harvey, and Rita Moreno, the film adaptation of the play, set in 1916 Mississippi, had what Maltin called "torrid performances making up for frequent staginess."[14] Alma was a great role for Ms. Page, who starred in the off-Broadway revival and received an Academy Award nomination for the film.

Sweet Bird of Youth (1962)

This film has strong performances by Geraldine Page as Alexandra the fading movie star, Paul Newman as Chance her ambitious gigolo, with supporting roles by Shirley Knight and Ed Begley as the corrupt town boss. Page and Knight received nominations for Best Actress and Supporting Actress, and Begley won the Oscar for Best Supporting Actor. It was written and directed by Richard Brooks.

Period of Adjustment (1962)

Williams subtitled this play "A Serious Comedy." Jane Fonda and Jim Hutton played the newlyweds, with Lois Nettleton and Tony Franciosa acting the older troubled couple they try to support. Maltin said the "engaging performers make the most of both comic and tender moments."[15] The director was George Roy Hill.

The Night of the Iguana (1964)

Veteran director John Huston tackled this troubling tale. A brilliant cast included Richard Burton as Reverend Shannon, Deborah Kerr as Hannah, Ava Gardner as Maxine, and Grayson Hall as Judith Fellows, the character who led the tour with Shannon. Grayson Hall won the Oscar for Best Supporting Actress, and costumer Dorothy Jeakins won her

Williams talks with famed director John Huston on the set of *The Night of the Iguana*, which was filmed on location in Mexico.

field's Oscar. Burton was already nominated that year for his lead role in Becket, so could not get a double nod. Maltin, not enthused about this version, called it "plodding."[16]

Ten Blocks on the Camino Real (1966)

Director Jack Landau filmed this play for the National Educational Television network. Starring young Martin Sheen as Kilroy, this expressionistic, sometimes surreal film also gives writing credit to Tennessee Williams, but it is unclear how much he contributed.

This Property Is Condemned (1966)

Fine performers Mary Badham, Natalie Wood, Robert Redford, Kate Reid, Robert Blake, and Charles Bronson, among others, fill out the large cast created from the poignant one-act play. Director Sydney Pollack and screenwriters including Francis Ford Coppola could not make a believable tale out of this slender story of the cruel abandonment of a brave child.

Boom! (1968)

British director Joseph Losey used locations in Sardinia and Rome to attempt to make this version of Williams's play *The Milk Train Doesn't Stop Here Anymore* a success. Performers Elizabeth Taylor, Richard Burton, Joanna Shimkus, and playwright Noel Coward failed to make a hit of this film of Williams's work.

Although these films are not perfect recreations of Williams's stage productions, they allow students to watch outstanding writers, directors, and designers at work on his material. They show us Williams's enduring characters played by some of the best, highly recognized actors to work in American theater and film.

Recent Revivals Show Williams's Staying Power

When Williams's plays are revived, critics, actors, and directors all have strong opinions about how they should be done. Often a critical debate explodes. These passionate, conflicting views show how important Williams's plays are in today's theater.

On March 23, 2005, a Broadway revival of *The Glass Menagerie* opened, directed by David Leveaux. An experienced director on London and New York stages, Leveaux decided to cast well-known film stars Jessica Lange as Amanda and Christian Slater as Tom. Lange, slim and attractive in her fifties, easily played the role as if Amanda were about forty-five. Slater had to move between the older Narrator and the twenty-something Tom.

The *New York Times* critic Ben Brantley did not buy their interpretation. He wrote about the "misdirected and miscast stars: the two-time Oscar winner Jessica Lange, who brings a sleepy neurotic sensuality to the role of the vital and domineering Amanda . . . and Christian Slater, who plays her poetical son Tom as a red-hot roughneck."[17] Critics from *Curtain Up* magazine said: "Despite the actors' often misguided mannerisms and line delivery, and the production's interesting but distracting look, it does all come together . . . "[18]

In an interview for *Playbill*, Lange said of her own plan for the role: "I made a deliberate decision not to play Amanda as some delusional relic of Southern gentility."[19] Lange tried to make her a woman easily understood by downtrodden, midlife mothers of today. Lange had the challenge of impressing critics who had recently seen Sally Field play Amanda in a Kennedy Center hit revival of the show in 2004.

Just as controversial was the revival of *A Streetcar Named Desire* on Broadway in April 2005. This production was directed by another Englishman, Edward Hall. It also featured actors that did not convince all the critics. Playing Blanche, film and stage star Natasha Richardson looked tall, youthful, and strong. Critics wondered why she needed to put paper lanterns over the lightbulbs, since her beauty was hardly fading. Critics also found John C. Reilly to be a stretch for their image of Stanley Kowalski. Eric Grode, critic for Broadway.com, said Reilly, who is noted for playing intense losers, "is the unlikeliest Stanley" since a musical cartoon version of the show appeared on *The Simpsons*.[20] Without a primitive, virile Stanley, Grode writes that "the sexual tension between Stanley and Blanche stays at an extremely low simmer."

Other critics praised Richardson (daughter of actress Vanessa Redgrave) for her performance. Clive Barnes wrote in the *New York Post* that Richardson "is a heaven-sent Blanche—a role she seems to have been born to play . . . her manner a mix of the shy, the sensuous, and the frankly sensual."[21]

About her approach to Blanche, Natasha Richardson said: "In playing someone who's in the midst of such pain and chaos, it's very necessary for me to have stability and order and calm in my own life. I've never before tackled anything of this size or range—period. . . . she is never offstage except for half a scene!"[22]

Tennessee Williams would have been pleased to see his plays continue to intrigue, entertain, and enlighten audiences around the world. Williams's plays are not only revived in North America and Europe but have become popular with Russian audiences. Dramaturg Christopher Baker, who has studied Williams productions in Russia, noted that the playwright is greatly respected in Moscow: "Now that censorship has been lifted, they have readapted his plays. His popularity has a new kick."[23]

Revivals of Williams plays continue every year. A typical revival of *Summer and Smoke* was slated for March 4 through April 17, 2016, at the Actors Co-op Theatre of Los Angeles. David C. Nichols wrote in his review: "The production avoids clichéd pitfalls and embraces the humanity that drives Williams' symbology-ridden study of the eternal clash between spirit and flesh . . . it unearths the mercurial yet specific qualities that make SMOKE a masterwork."[24]

Revivals of Williams's plays continue to draw new audiences in the United States and around the world. Here a marquee announces a 2013 Broadway production of *The Glass Menagerie*.

Tennessee Williams only wanted to write and have his writing enjoyed. In the spring of 1982, he wrote to his close friend Maria St. Just who lived in England: "I have a play opening in Chicago on Tuesday [April 27]: am casting another play in New York on the 28th, something for the "Miami Festival"—I have a play that I want to develop, so there I'll go."[25] In May 1982, he complained to St. Just that his American agents were not trying to get him new American productions: "Well, my dear girl, I must suspend these rather bleak communications pour le moment and do a bit of work on a play called *The Lingering Hour*— the twilight of the world which I hope I am managing to make somewhat poetic despite its subject matter. With all my love, Tennessee."[26]

> **dramaturg**
>
> Member of a theater organization that prepares the script for performance regarding translations, updated versions, and historical background. During production, the dramaturg advises directors and designers about the playwright's intentions.

Williams never completed this play before his accidental death in February 1983. Yet he need not have been concerned about his work being produced in his native country or anywhere else in the theater world. Tennessee Williams said he was his work —and his work still lives. His creative genius will certainly draw audiences to stage and screen for many generations to come.

CHRONOLOGY

1911– Thomas Lanier Williams III is born on March 26 in Columbus, Mississippi.
Tom, mother Edwina, and sister Rose live with grandparents while father Cornelius sells on the road.

1914–1915– Reverend Walter and Grandmother Isabel Dakin move to Nashville, Tennessee, and then Clarksdale, Mississippi. Tom and his family come along.

1916– Tom is seriously ill with diphtheria and a kidney infection.

1918– Cornelius Williams moves his wife and children to St. Louis permanently.

1919– Williams's brother Dakin is born; Edwina contracts influenza.

1920– Williams leaves St. Louis to spend time with grandparents in Clarksdale, Mississippi.

1921– Returns to St. Louis to live with his parents and complete his schooling. At age twelve, gets his first typewriter.

1925– Rose is sent to Vicksburg for private school; onset of her behavior and emotional problems.

1927– Williams attends University City High School and wins first writing award, from *Smart Set* magazine.

1928– Goes on European tour with grandfather. *Weird Tales* magazine buys his first story.

1929– Enrolls at University of Missouri at Columbia. Audits playwriting class; studies dramatists; completes three years. Publishes poetry.

1931– Clerks at International Shoe on and off for several years.

1932– Quits University of Missouri at his father's insistence.

1935– Suffers collapse from exhaustion, nerves, and depression. Resigns from International Shoe; spends six months with grandparents in Memphis; has first short play produced in June.

1936— Enrolls at Washington University in St. Louis, studies literature. One-act play "The Magic Tower" is produced by Webster Groves Theatre Guild.

1937— Enrolls at State University of Iowa.

1938— Completes bachelors degree in theater at University of Iowa in August. Completes two full-length plays in workshop. Applies for scholarship to return but is denied. Revises his full-length play, *Not About Nightingales*. (Not produced until 1998.) The Mummers theater in St. Louis produces *Fugitive Kind*.

1939— Lives in New Orleans, starts sending out stories and plays as "Tennessee Williams." First one with this name on it is published in *Story Magazine*.

1940— Accepted in New School's Dramatic Workshop, New York. Writes *Battle of Angels*; works on *Stairs to the Roof*.

1941— *Battle of Angels* gets first professional production in Boston, but fails.

1942–1944— Writes plays; lives off grants, part-time jobs, one stint as Hollywood scriptwriter, charity of family and friends.

1944— Grandmother Dakin dies in Edwina's home. *The Glass Menagerie* opens in Chicago in December.

1945— *The Glass Menagerie* is a hit on Broadway. Works on *A Streetcar Named Desire, Stairs to the Roof*.

1946— Works on *A Streetcar Named Desire, Summer and Smoke, Camino Real*.

1947— *Summer and Smoke* opens in Dallas. *Stairs to the Roof* opens at Pasadena Playhouse, California. *A Streetcar Named Desire* opens on Broadway, wins Pulitzer and New York Drama Critics Circle award. Parents permanently separate.

1948— *Summer and Smoke* opens on Broadway. Frank Merlo becomes Williams's assistant and lover for fourteen years.

1949 – Discovers Key West, writes *The Rose Tattoo*.
1950 – *The Roman Spring of Mrs. Stone* is published.
The Rose Tattoo opens in Chicago. Film of *The Glass Menagerie* released.
1951 – *The Rose Tattoo* opens on Broadway, wins Tony Award.
1952 – Film of *A Streetcar Named Desire* is released. Works on *Camino Real*. *Summer and Smoke* runs off Broadway.
1953 – *Camino Real* opens on Broadway. Writes *Cat on a Hot Tin Roof*.
1954 – *The Rose Tattoo* films in Key West.
1955 – Grandfather Dakin dies in February. *Cat on a Hot Tin Roof* opens on Broadway.
Writes screenplay for *Baby Doll*.
1956 – *Sweet Bird of Youth* opens in Miami. Serious trouble with Merlo, Williams near nervous breakdown. Mother is committed to psychiatric ward; Williams flees to Virgin Islands.
1957 – Keeps mother in Key West; writes *Orpheus Descending*. Cornelius Williams dies in May. Williams attends funeral. Undergoes psychotherapy in New York.
1958 – *Something Unspoken* and *Suddenly Last Summer* open off Broadway.
Writes *Period of Adjustment*. Film of *Cat on a Hot Tin Roof* is released.
1959 – *Sweet Bird of Youth* opens on Broadway. *I Rise in Flames, Cried the Phoenix* opens off Broadway.
1960 – Writes *The Night of the Iguana* in Key West. *Period of Adjustment* opens on Broadway. Film of *Orpheus Descending*, called *The Fugitive Kind*, is released.
1961 – *The Night of the Iguana* opens on Broadway.
1963 – *Milk Train Doesn't Stop Here* opens off Broadway. Merlo dies of cancer in New York.
1964 – Writes *Slapstick Tragedy*. Film of *The Night of the Iguana* released.
1966 – *Slapstick Tragedy* opens in New York.

1968— *The Seven Descents of Myrtle* opens on Broadway. Film of *The Milk Train Doesn't Stop Here*, called *BOOM!*, is released.

1969— Mental health declines. Dakin has Williams baptized Roman Catholic in Key West. Attempts suicide with sleeping pills. *In the Bar of a Tokyo Hotel* opens in New York. Has a breakdown. Dakin commits Williams to St. Louis hospital for detoxification and psychiatric treatment.

1971— Breaks with thirty-two-year agent, Audrey Wood. *Out Cry* opens in Chicago, then in New York.

1972— *Small Craft Warnings* opens off Broadway. Williams sometimes plays a role.

1973— *Out Cry* opens in New York. Spends year touring Far East.

1974— *Out Cry* opens off Broadway, but fails. Broadway revival of *Cat on a Hot Tin Roof* is huge success.

1975— Four major revivals are hits in New York and Washington. Works on *Red Devil Battery Sign*; briefly produced in Boston. Williams's book *Memoirs* is published.

1976— November: *Eccentricities of a Nightingale* opens in New York, but fails. Is made lifetime member of American Academy of Arts and Letters.

1978— *Vieux Carré* is a hit in London.

1979— *A Lovely Sunday for Creve Coeur* opens off Broadway. Receives the Kennedy Center Award for the Arts on December 2.

1980— *Clothes for a Summer Hotel* opens on Broadway. Mother Edwina dies at age ninety-five. Receives Presidential Medal of Freedom, highest civilian award. Becomes Distinguished Writer in Residence at University of British Columbia.

1981— *Something Cloudy, Something Clear*, an autobiographical play, opens off Broadway successfully.

1982– *A House Not Meant to Stand* opens in Chicago. Receives Honorary Doctor of Letters degree from Harvard. Works on adaptation of *The Seagull* by Chekhov, other new works.

1983– Dies at Hotel Elysée in New York on February 24, has medicine bottle top lodged in throat. His death is judged an accident. Broadway theaters all dim their lights in his memory.

1994– Honored by a US Postal Service stamp.

1998– *Not About Nightingales* premieres at the Royal National Theatre in London, and later moves to the Alley Theatre in Houston, Texas.

1999– *Spring Storm* premieres at the Actors Repertory of Texas in Austin. *Not About Nightingales* plays on Broadway.

2000–2010– The following works receive publication: *The Selected Letters Vol 1, Stairs to the Roof, Fugitive Kind, Collected Poems, Candles to the Sun, The Selected Letters Vol 2, Notebooks, A House Not Meant to Stand, The Traveling Companion, New Selected Essays: Where I Live,* and *The Magic Tower.*

2011– Centennial of Williams's birth. Among the many worldwide productions, the Comedie-Française produces *Un tramway nomme Desir*, the first play by a non-European author in the company's 331-year history.

CHAPTER NOTES

Chapter 1. From Storyteller to Poet to Playwright

1. Lyle Leverich, *Tom: The Unknown Tennessee Williams* (New York: W. W. Norton & Company, 1995), 249.
2. Ronald Hayman, *Tennessee Williams: Everyone Else Is Just an Audience* (New Haven: Yale University Press, 1993), 10.
3. Leverich, 10.
4. Ibid., 105.
5. Ibid., 119.
6. Ibid.
7. Ibid., 130.
8. Ibid., 160.
9. Ibid., 48.
10. Ibid., 149.
11. Ibid., 153.
12. Donald Spoto, *The Kindness of Strangers: The Life of Tennessee Williams* (Boston: Little, Brown and Co., 1985), 55.
13. Leverich, 226.
14. Tennessee Williams, *The Fugitive Kind* (New York: New Directions Books, University of the South, 2001), 106.
15. Ibid., 124.
16. Leverich, 132.
17. Spoto, 15.

Chapter 2. Building a Playwright's Résumé

1. Tennessee Williams, *In the Winter of Cities* (New York: New Directions, 1952), 76.
2. Ronald Hayman, *Tennessee Williams: Everyone Else Is an Audience* (Yale University Press, 1993), 53.
3. Laura Kepley, speaking at Trinity Repertory Theatre, Providence, Rhode Island, October 29, 2005.
4. Tennessee Williams, *27 Wagons Full of Cotton and Other One-Act Plays* (New York: New Directions, 1945), 69.
5. Ibid., 70.
6. Ibid., 190.
7. Ibid., 193.

8. Ibid., 199.

9. Karen Bovard, "Lost in the Funhouse: New Life for Some Neglected One-Acts by Tennessee Williams," *Hartford Advocate*, October 19, 2003, http://www. hartfordadvocate.com/gbase/arts.

10. Donald Spoto, *The Kindness of Strangers: The Life of Tennessee Williams* (Boston: Little Brown, 1985), 6.

11. Lyle Leverich, *Tom: The Unknown Tennessee Williams* (New York: W. W. Norton & Company, 1995), 436.

12. Tennessee Williams, *Memoirs* (New York: Doubleday and Company, 1975), 85.

13. Robert A. Martin, ed., reviews reprinted in *Critical Essays on Tennessee Williams* (New York: G. K. Hall & Co., 1997), 197.

14. John Lahr, *Tennessee Williams: Mad Pilgrimage of the Flesh* (New York: W. W. Norton, 2014), 7.

15. Leverich, 554.

16. Esther M. Jackson, "Tennessee Williams: The Idea of a 'Plastic Form,'" reprinted in *Critical Essays on Tennessee Williams*, Robert A. Martin, ed. (New York: G. K. Hall & Co., 1997), 197.

17. Williams, *Memoirs*, 84–85.

18. Albert J. Devlin, ed., *Conversations With Tennessee Williams* (Jackson, MS: University Press of Mississippi, 1986), 10.

19. Tennessee Williams, *The Glass Menagerie*, in *The Theatre of Tennessee Williams*, vol. 1 (New York: New Directions Books, 1971), 163.

20. Williams, *Memoirs*, 48.

21. Williams, *The Glass Menagerie*, 159.

22. Ibid., 237.

23. Ibid., 228.

24. Ibid., 164.

25. Lincoln Barnett, "Tennessee Williams," *Life*, February 16, 1948, 116.

26. Roger Boxill, *Tennessee Williams* (New York: St. Martins Press, 1987), 22.

27. Judith J. Thompson, *Tennessee Williams' Plays: Memory, Myth, and Symbol* (New York: Peter Lang, 1989), 14.

28. Martin, 19–24.

Chapter 3. A Ride on the *Streetcar*, A *Summer* of Smoke

1. Tennessee Williams, *New Selected Essays: Where I Live* (New York: New Directions, 2009), 42.

2. Donald Spoto, *The Kindness of Strangers: The Life of Tennessee Williams* (Boston: Little, Brown and Company, 1985), 118.

3. John Lahr, *Tennessee Williams: Mad Pilgrimage of the Flesh* (New York: W. W. Norton, 2015), 69.

4. Ronald Hayman, *Tennessee Williams: Everyone Else Is an Audience* (Yale University Press, 1993), 103.

5. Lahr, 141.

6. Tennessee Williams, *Memoirs* (New York: Doubleday & Co., 1975), 131.

7. Louise Blackwell, "Tennessee Williams and the Predicament of Women," in *Tennessee Williams: A Collection of Essays*, Stephen S. Stanton, ed. (Upper Saddle River, NJ: Prentice Hall, 1977), 100.

8. Chris Jones, "Sex in the Big Easy," *Front & Center Magazine*, Spring 2005, 6.

9. Ibid.

10. Tennessee Williams, "A Streetcar Named Desire" in *The Theatre of Tennessee Williams*, vol. 1 (New York: New Directions Books, 1971), 323.

11. Ibid., 351.

12. Ibid., 332.

13. Judith J. Thompson, *Tennessee Williams' Plays: Memory, Myth, and Symbol* (New York: Peter Lang, 1989), 41.

14. Williams, *A Streetcar Named Desire*, 323.

15. Kimball King, "The Rebirth of *Orpheus Descending*," in *Critical Essays on Tennessee Williams*, Robert A. Martin, ed. (New York: G. K. Hall & Co., 1997), 140.

16. Martin, reviews reprinted in *Critical Essays on Tennessee Williams*, 25–30.

17. Williams, *Memoirs*, 156.

18. Spoto, 153.

19. *Five O'Clock Angel: Letters of Tennessee Williams to Maria St. Just 1948–1982*, with commentary by Maria St. Just (New York: Alfred A. Knopf, 1990), 14.

20. Donald Windham, ed., *Tennessee Williams's Letters to Donald Windham 1940–1965* (Athens, GA: University of Georgia Press, 1996), 225.

21. Thomas P. Adler, "Before the Fall—and After," *The Cambridge Companion to Tennessee Williams*, Matthew C. Roudane, ed. (Cambridge University Press, 1997), 116.

22. Tennessee Williams, *Summer and Smoke* in *The Theatre of Tennessee Williams*, vol. II (New York: New Directions Books, 1971), 202.

23. Ibid., 221.

24. Ibid., 243.

25. Ibid., 241.

26. Brooks Atkinson, *The New York Times*, October 7, 1948, 33.

27. Authors Note by Williams, *The Theatre of Tennessee Williams*, 7.

28. Tennessee Williams, *Eccentricities of a Nightingale* in *The Theatre of Tennessee Williams*, vol. II (New York: New Directions, 1971), 104.

29. Ibid., 110.

30. Spoto, 179–180.

Chapter 4. The Shocking Duality of the Single Heart

1. John Lahr, *Tennessee Williams: Mad Pilgrimage of the Flesh* (New York: W. W. Norton, 2015), 311–312.

2. Ronald Hayman, *Tennessee Williams: Everyone Else Is an Audience* (Yale University Press, 1993), 131.

3. Donald Windham, ed., *Tennessee Williams's Letters to Donald Windham 1940–1965* (Athens, GA: University of Georgia Press, 1996), 249.

4. Arthur B. Waters, "Tennessee Williams: Ten Years Later," *Conversations with Tennessee Williams*, Albert J. Devlin, ed. (Jackson, MS: University Press of Mississippi, 1986), 35.

5. Ibid.

6. Tennessee Williams, *Cat on a Hot Tin Roof*, in *The Theatre of Tennessee Williams*, vol. III (New York: New Directions, 1975), 117.

7. Ibid., 119.

8. Ibid.

9. Ibid., 26.

10. Ibid., 53.

11. Dianne Cafagna, "Blanche DuBois and Maggie the Cat: Illusion and Reality in Tennessee Williams," in *Critical Essays on Tennessee Williams*, Robert A. Martin, ed. (New York: G. K. Hall & Co., 1997), 122.

12. Williams, *Cat on a Hot Tin Roof*, 61.

13. Ibid., 124.

14. Judith J. Thompson, *Tennessee Williams' Plays: Memory, Myth, and Symbol* (New York: Peter Lang Publishing, 1989), 81.

15. Brooks Atkinson, "Theatre: Tennessee Williams's 'Cat,'" *The New York Times*, March 25, 1955, 18.

16. Ibid.

17. Robert Coleman, *New York Daily Mirror*, March 25, 1955, 21, reprinted in *Critical Essays on Tennessee Williams*, 45.

18. Ibid.

19. Lizzie Loveridge, "A Curtain Up Review: *Cat on a Hot Tin Roof*," accessed August 11, 2006, http://www.curtainup.com/catonahottineroof.

Chapter 5. Restless Roaming in the Fifties

1. Lewis Funke and John E. Booth, 1962 interview, in *Conversations with Tennessee Williams*, Albert Devlin, ed. (Jackson, MS: University Press of Mississippi, 1986), 104.

2. Tennessee Williams, *The Rose Tattoo* in *The Theatre of Tennessee Williams*, vol. II (New York: New Directions, 1971), 278.

3. Tennessee Williams, *Something Cloudy, Something Clear* (New York: New Directions, 1995), 23.

4. Nancy Tischler, "Romantic Textures in Tennessee Williams' Plays and Short Stories," *Cambridge Companion to Tennessee Williams*, Matthew C. Roudane, ed. (Cambridge: Cambridge University Press), 147.

5. Williams, *The Rose Tattoo*, 329.

6. Brooks Atkinson, *The New York Times*, February 5, 1951, 33.

7. Ibid.

8. Williams, *The Rose Tattoo*, 341.

9. Ibid., 403.

10. John Lahr, *Tennessee Williams: Mad Pilgrimage of the Flesh* (New York: W. W. Norton, 2015), 193.

11. Tennessee Williams, *Night of the Iguana*, in *The Theatre of Tennessee Williams*, vol. IV (New York: New Directions, 1972), 302.
12. Ibid., 373.
13. Ibid., 367-368.
14. Quoted by Thomas P. Adler, *Cambridge Companion to Tennessee Williams*, 121.
15. Howard Taubman, "Theatre: Night of the Iguana Opens," *The New York Times*, December 29, 1961, 10.
16. Ibid.
17. Tennessee Williams, "A Summer of Discovery," *Where I Live: Selected Essays*, Christine R. Day and Bob Woods, eds. (New York: New Directions, 1978), 123.

Chapter 6. Notable Works Take On Poetic Themes

1. Tennessee Williams, Foreword to *Sweet Bird of Youth*, in *The Theatre of Tennessee Williams*, vol. IV (New York: New Directions, 1972), 6.
2. Tennessee Williams, Foreword to *Camino Real* (New York: New Directions, 1953), ix.
3. Tennessee Williams, *Suddenly Last Summer* in *The Theatre of Tennessee Williams*, vol. III (New York: New Directions, 1971), 349.
4. Ibid., 363.
5. Ibid., 421.
6. Ibid., 423.
7. Bosley Crowther, "*Suddenly Last Summer;* Movie From Williams Play at 2 Houses Elizabeth Taylor and Clift Head Cast," *The New York Times*, December 23, 1959.
8. Williams, *Sweet Bird of Youth*, 9.
9. Ibid., 118.
10. Ibid., 199.
11. Ibid., 124.
12. John Lahr, *Tennessee Williams: Mad Pilgrimage of the Flesh* (New York: W. W. Norton, 2015), 395.
13. Ibid., 463.
14. Tennessee Williams, *Memoirs* (New York: Doubleday and Company, 1975), p. 189.
15. Ibid., 194.
16. Ibid., 203.

17. Philip C. Kolin, *The Influence of Tennessee Williams: Essays on Fifteen American Playwrights* (Jefferson, NC: McFarland, 2008), 5.
18. Tennessee Williams, *Small Craft Warnings* (New York: New Directions, 1970), 15.
19. William Prosser, *The Late Plays of Tennessee Williams*, (Lanham, MD: Scarecrow Press, 2009), vi.
20. Tennessee Williams, *Red Devil Battery Sign* (New York: New Directions, 1975), 62.
21. Albert J. Devlin, ed., "Roundtable: Tennessee Williams, Craig Anderson, and T. E. Kalem Talk About *Creve Coeur*," *Conversations With Tennessee Williams* (Jackson, MS: University Press of Mississippi, 1986), 310.
22. Ibid., 311.
23. Ibid., 313.
24. Ibid., 316.
25. Dotson Rader, *Tennessee: Cry of the Heart* (New York: Doubleday & Co., 1985), 298.
26. Ibid., 360.

Chapter 7. How Great Playwrights Influence Each Other

1. Tennessee Williams, *Notebooks: Tennessee Williams*, Margaret Bradham Thornton, ed. (New Haven, CT: Yale University Press, 2006), quoted in John Lahr, *Tennessee Williams: Mad Pilgrimage of the Flesh* (New York: W. W. Norton, 2015), 96.
2. Ibid.
3. Tennessee Williams, *Memoirs* (New York: Doubleday and Company, 1975), 41.
4. Ibid., 40.
5. Ibid., 41.
6. Oscar Brockett and Robert J. Ball, *The Essential Theatre*, 8th ed. (Wadsworth/Thompson Learning, 2004), 165.
7. Peter Arnott, *The Theatre in Its Time* (Boston: Little, Brown & Co., 1981), 366.
8. Dotson Rader, *Tennessee: Cry of the Heart* (New York: Doubleday and Co., 1985), 285.
9. "About William Inge," William Inge Center for the Arts, accessed July 1, 2016 http://www.ingecenter.org/aboutinge.html.

10. Quoted in Philip C. Kolin, *The Influence of Tennessee Williams: Essays on Fifteen American Playwrights* (Jefferson, NC: McFarland, 2008), 17.
11. "About William Inge," 1.
12. Rader, 326.
13. Ronald Hayman, *Tennessee Williams: Everyone Else Is an Audience* (New Haven, CT: Yale University Press, 1993), 98.
14. Raymond Williams, "Arthur Miller: An Overview," *Arthur Miller*, Harold Bloom, ed. (New York: Chelsea House, 1987), 13.
15. Mel Gussow, *Edward Albee: A Singular Journey* (New York: Simon & Schuster, 1999), 92.
16. Charles S. Krohn and Julian N. Wasserman, "An Interview With Edward Albee," March 18, 1981, in *Edward Albee: An Interview and Essays* (Houston, TX: University of St. Thomas, 1983), 2.
17. Edward Albee, *Who's Afraid of Virginia Woolf?* (New York: Atheneum, 1978), 190–191.
18. David Crespy, "Inconspicuous Osmosis and the Plasticity of Doing Edward Albee," quoted in Philip C. Kolin, *The Influence of Tennessee Williams: Essays on Fifteen American Playwrights* (Jefferson, NC: McFarland, 2008), 48.

Chapter 8. Williams's Work Lives On

1. Quoted in John Lahr, *Tennessee Williams: Mad Pilgrimage of the Flesh* (New York: W. W. Norton, 2015), 559.
2. Leonard Maltin, *Leonard Maltin's Classic Movie Guide* (New York: Plume, 2015), 254.
3. Leonard Maltin, *Leonard Maltin's Movie & Video Guide 1997 Edition* (New York: Signet Books, 1996), 509.
4. R. Barton Palmer, "Hollywood in Crisis: Tennessee Williams and the Evolution of the Adult Film," *The Cambridge Companion to Tennessee Williams*, Matthew C. Roudane, ed. (Cambridge: Cambridge University Press, 1997), 214.
5. *Leonard Maltin's Classic Movie Guide*, 668.
6. Ibid.
7. *Leonard Maltin's Movie & Video Guide*, 1285.
8. *Leonard Maltin's Classic Movie Guide*, 668.
9. Ibid., 586.
10. Ibid., 34.

11. Ibid., 110.

12. Ibid., 672.

13. Ibid., 238.

14. Ibid., 672.

15. Ibid., 530.

16. Ibid., 489.

17. Ben Brantley, "Theatre Review: A 'Menagerie' Full of Stars, Silhouettes, and Weird Sounds," accessed May 13, 2005, http:// theatre2nytimes. com/mem/theater/review.

18. "A Curtain Up Review: *The Glass Menagerie*," accessed May 13, 2015, http://www.curtainup.com/glassmenageriebway.

19. C. F. Kane, "Amanda for All Seasons," *Playbill*, March 2005, 54.

20. Eric Grode, *A Streetcar Named Desire*, accessed May 13, 2005, http:// www.broadway.com/gen/Buzz.

21. Clive Barnes, *A Streetcar Named Desire*, accessed May 13, 2005, http:// www.broadway.com/gen/Buzz_Story.

22. Jerry Tallmer, "Darkness Becomes Her," *Playbill*, April 2005, 26.

23. Christopher Baker, interview with the author at the Hartford Stage Company, Hartford, CT, December 20, 2005.

24. David C. Nichols, "Summer and Smoke" review, *Los Angeles Times*, March 12, 2016.

25. *Five O'Clock Angel: Letters of Tennessee Williams to Maria St. Just 1948–1982* (New York: Alfred A. Knopf, 1990), 388.

26. Ibid., 390.

Literary Terms

canon—The complete list of books by any author regarded as authentically his work.

diphtheria—A contagious bacterial disease that attacks the throat, nose, nerves, and heart. Children are now vaccinated against it.

Dramatist Guild of America—Organization that promotes and protects the professional interests of playwrights, composers, lyricists, and librettists.

dramaturg—Member of a theater organization that prepares the script for performance regarding translations, updated versions, and historical background. During production, the dramaturg advises directors and designers about the playwright's intentions.

Group Theatre—Formed in 1931 in New York, this company held left-wing political views and produced plays that explored social issues.

irony—The incongruity of an expected situation (or its outcome) and the actual situation (or its outcome). In language, irony is the deliberate use of words to contrast an apparent meaning with the words' intended meaning (which are usually the complete opposite of each other).

metaphor—An implied comparison achieved by using a word or phrase not in its literal sense, but as an analogy. Example (from Shakespeare): "Life's but a walking shadow, a poor player that struts and frets his hour upon the stage."

monologue (internal or interior)—A long speech by an

individual character in which he lets the audience alone know his inner thoughts and feelings.

monologue (external or exterior)—A long speech by an individual character, sometimes in the presence of other characters, that reveals his past or planned actions and intentions.

New York Drama Critics Circle—Theater critics from all the New York City newspapers and magazines except for the *New York Times*, who vote on the Best Play, Best Musical, and Best Foreign Play each year on Broadway.

pathos—An element in creative art or experience that evokes sympathy, pity, and/ or compassion.

realism—A style of writing in which the subject is represented as it would be in real life.

symbol—Something that stands for, represents, or suggests another thing.

symbolism—The representation of things by use of symbols.

Theatre Guild—Founded in 1919 in New York, this producing group was owned by its board of directors, which included playwrights, actors, and designers. It was noted for giving new authors a chance to develop. Some younger radical members broke away and formed the Group Theatre.

theme—A distinctive quality or concern in one or more works of fiction.

Major Works by
Tennessee Williams

Fugitive Kind (1937)
Not About Nightingales (1938; produced 1998)
Battle of Angels (1941)
The Glass Menagerie (1944)
Summer and Smoke (1947)
Stairs to the Roof (1947)
A Streetcar Named Desire (1947)
The Rose Tattoo (1950)
The Roman Spring of Mrs. Stone (1950)
Camino Real (1953)
Cat on a Hot Tin Roof (1955)
Baby Doll (1955)
Sweet Bird of Youth (1956)
Orpheus Descending (1957)
Something Unspoken (1958)
Suddenly Last Summer (1958)
Period of Adjustment (1958)
I Rise in Flames, Cried the Phoenix (1959)
The Night of the Iguana (1960)
The Milk Train Doesn't Stop Here (1962)
Slapstick Tragedy (1964)
The Seven Descents of Myrtle (1968)
Boom! (1968)
In the Bar of a Tokyo Hotel (1969)
Out Cry (1971)
Small Craft Warnings (1972)
Memoirs (1975)
Eccentricities of a Nightingale (1976)
Vieux Carre (1977)
Red Devil Battery Sign (1977)

A Lovely Sunday for Creve Coeur (1978)
Clothes for a Summer Hotel (1980)
Something Cloudy, Something Clear (1981)
A House Not Meant to Stand (1982)

Further Reading

Books

Grissom, James. *Follies of God: Tennessee Williams and the Women of the Fog.* New York: Knopf, 2015.

Kolin, Philip. *The Tennessee Williams Encyclopedia.* Westport, CT: Greenwood, 2004.

Lahr, John. *Tennessee Williams: Mad Pilgrimage of the Flesh.* New York: W. W. Norton, 2014.

Roudané, Matthew C. *The Cambridge Companion to Tennessee Williams.* Boston: Cambridge University Press, 1998.

Tischler, Nancy M. *Student Companion to Tennessee Williams.* Westport, CT: Greenwood, 2000.

Websites

The Tennessee Williams/New Orleans Literary Festival
www.tennesseewilliams.net/
An annual celebration of the works of Williams as well as the rich cultural heritage of the New Orleans area.

The Mississippi Writers Page: Tennessee Williams
mwp.olemiss.edu//dir/williams_tennessee/index.html
Includes biography, publications, productions, and resources related to Williams.

Poetry Foundation: Tennessee Williams
www.poetryfoundation.org/poems-and-poets/poets/detail/tennessee-williams#poet
Provides a detailed analysis of Williams's life and work as well as links to poetry and audio clips.

INDEX